J O U R N E Y TO
SIGNIFICANCE

How to break free from mediocre faith and discover
your road map to purpose and fulfillment

TONY MILLER

Charisma
HOUSE

JOURNEY TO SIGNIFICANCE by Tony Miller
Published by Charisma House
A part of Strang Communications Company
600 Rinehart Road
Lake Mary, Florida 32746
www.charismahouse.com

This book or parts thereof may not be reproduced in any form, stored in a retrieval system or transmitted in any form by any means—electronic, mechanical, photocopy, recording or otherwise—without prior written permission of the publisher, except as provided by United States of America copyright law.

Unless otherwise noted, all Scripture quotations are from the New King James Version of the Bible. Copyright © 1979, 1980, 1982 by Thomas Nelson, Inc., publishers. Used by permission.

Scripture quotations marked AMP are from the Amplified Bible. Old Testament copyright © 1965, 1987 by the Zondervan Corporation. The Amplified New Testament copyright © 1954, 1958, 1987 by the Lockman Foundation. Used by permission.

Scripture quotations marked KJV are from the King James Version of the Bible.

Scripture quotations marked NAS are from the New American Standard Bible. Copyright © 1960, 1962, 1963, 1968, 1971, 1972, 1973, 1975, 1977 by the Lockman Foundation. Used by permission. (www.Lockman.org)

Scripture quotations marked NIV are from the Holy Bible, New International Version. Copyright © 1973, 1978, 1984, International Bible Society. Used by permission.

Scripture quotations marked NLT are from the Holy Bible, New Living Translation, copyright © 1996. Used by permission of Tyndale House Publishers, Inc., Wheaton, IL 60189. All rights reserved.

Scripture quotations marked TLB are from The Living Bible. Copyright © 1971. Used by permission of Tyndale House Publishers, Inc., Wheaton, IL 60189. All rights reserved.

Scripture quotations marked THE MESSAGE are from *The Message*, copyright 1993, 1994, 1995. Used by permission of NavPress Publishing Group.

Cover design by Debbie Lewis
Interior design by David Bilby

Copyright © 2003 by Tony Miller
All rights reserved

Library of Congress Cataloging-in-Publication Data:

Miller, Tony, 1957–
    Journey to significance / Tony Miller.
        p. cm.
    ISBN 0-88419-877-4 (trade paper)
    1. Christian life. 2. Life--Religious aspects--Christianity. I. Title.
    BV4501.3.M55 2003
    248.4--dc21
                                    2002154679

    03 04 05 06 07 — 8 7 6 5 4 3 2 1
            Printed in the United States of America

To my beautiful bride, Kathy J. Miller, whom this year I have had the privilege of calling my wife for twenty-five years.

Kathy, you are the most real, genuine person I know. Your passion for the Lord and dreams you carry are unequaled. You have always had the ability to ignite the flames of desire and creativity in those around you, encouraging them to become something they never thought they could be. While many have warmed their spirits with your counsel, the embers you have most often fanned into flame and guarded have been mine.

I dedicate this book to you because you knew me when our journey was rocked by uncertainty, our dreams seemed frail, our finances were low, and my faith in God and myself were on trial. It is from the life that we have shared together that the truths of this book have been forged. Together we have survived the winds of life that have sought to blow us off course and the hazards of being out front in leadership, having to deal with expectations of those around who believe you are divine while you are in the midst of struggling with your own humanity. You are tough and tender. You have raised our children while I have traveled the globe, spending nights alone, just you and God, making choices for our future.

Kathy, if I had to start the journey all over again, I would still choose you as my partner. I know of no one who compares to your commitment to me or our mandate from Him. You continually call me higher...to that place of significance. You really are the "wind beneath my wings"!

acknowledgments

There are many wonderful people who have contributed in innumerable ways to the writing of this book and my experience in learning to make the journey.

I will be eternally grateful to my family, who generously shares me with the world on a continual basis without hints of selfishness or resentment. Your love and support have been a bedrock of strength to me throughout my life, especially in the writing of this book. From my parents who taught me to value the purpose of God on my life, to my wife who champions the assignment on my life, to my children who constantly remind me what this is really all about. All of you are a testimony of the greatness God puts in our lives. Thank you for continually believing in the dream we share together.

My heart is full of appreciation to my church family and colaborers, with whom I have shared so much of my journey. Your compassion and encouragement have meant so much in my life. Thanks for believing in me when others did not.

Thanks to my Destiny Team, who tirelessly labor to enhance the stewardship that has been entrusted to us with their insights and creativity. You guys are the greatest!

Special thanks to J. Lee Grady, who saw the potential of this project and continued to pursue it until it became a reality. Your enthusiasm is contagious!

Thank you to the wonderful people at Strang Communications who have treated me so graciously, working with my schedule and transitions, while treating my work with respect and integrity. I am especially grateful for Barbara Dycus and Ann Mulchan, who have been there for me throughout this project, and everyone at Charisma House who works to make this information available to the world.

contents

I n the fall of 2002 I was invited to speak at a conference in Idaho. When I arrived, the person who organized the event surprised me with an unusual gift to show her appreciation: a slingshot, accompanied by five smooth stones. Along with it, she gave me a card with a beautiful illustration of a young David preparing to slay Goliath.

I framed the picture of the young warrior, and today I keep it in my office—along with the slingshot and the shiny rocks. It is a daily reminder that I am called to face my giants with courage and faith. It also reminds me that all of life is a battlefield and that the man or woman God uses must learn to overcome obstacles if they expect success.

You have to understand that I didn't grow up thinking of myself as a giant killer. I was never the first kid to be picked for the kickball game. I considered myself a loser. I quickly learned to disqualify myself because I felt inferior when compared to other kids. And when I grew up, my childhood inadequacies developed into adult-sized insecurities. I didn't feel destined for success. I certainly didn't think I was on a journey to significance.

But all that began to change after I had an encounter with the Holy Spirit twenty-seven years ago. He began to deal with my heart, releasing me from the fears, doubts and lies that held me in a prison of spiritual mediocrity. He taught me that He could be glorified even in my weaknesses. I soon began to realize that God had indeed called me to fight—and to win.

I have faced more than a few Goliaths since then, and I know I will face more. One thing I know from my limited experience of giant-slaying is this: We can't overcome devilish obstacles if we are listening to the voices of doubt and criticism that are all around us. To arise as true warriors, we must tap into the voice of faith and find the encouragement that flows from God's heart to us.

I have found that kind of invigorating encouragement in my friend Tony Miller, and that's why I asked him back in 2001 to write this book. Tony reminds me of the apostle known as Barnabas in the Book of Acts. He is a "son of encouragement." When everyone else tells me to pack it up or get out of the battle, Tony tells me to fight on. Like a skilled coach, he knows how to bring out the best in a person, no matter how many times they have failed or how they bungled the last game.

I remember one of the first times I heard Tony preach in a church. I was so stirred by his message that I went to the altar when the meeting was over and asked him to pray for me. Tony spoke some encouraging things to my heart, telling me that God was pleased with my boldness in the face of criticism. He also prayed that God would grant me spiritual refreshment and renewal at a time when I was contemplating a major life decision.

But then he did something very unusual. He picked me up off the ground, walked about five feet to his left, and then set me down! The other people standing near the altar must have been amused at this odd display, but I wasn't laughing. I suddenly felt overcome by the Holy Spirit's power, and I heard the Lord speak directly to my heart after Tony did this. "Let Me move you where I want you," I heard the Lord say. "You don't have to struggle or strive in your own ability. Wait on Me. When it is My time, I will move you."

I will never forget that moment. And when I face discouragement and difficult circumstances, I often recall those words. And because of that moment I will always value Tony Miller as a source of inspiration and encouragement when I am going through tough times.

After I got to know Tony and heard his life message, I told him he needed to write it in book form because he can't possibly travel to all the places in the world where people need this kind of life-giving encouragement. Everywhere I go, I find Christians who have been crippled by life's pain and disappointments. Unfortunately, the people around them aren't calling them out of their despair. Often, discouraged people simply learn to live in their pit of broken dreams. And sadly, they don't always find help at church— because so many discouraged people are hiding there!

If you grasp the message of *Journey to Significance*, you will not only learn to crawl out of your pit, but you will discover the joy of pulling others out, too. I hope that when you finish this book, you won't hold on to it. Share it with a discouraged friend. Give it to a battle-weary warrior. Loan it to a pastor who has been sidelined by failure. Give it to someone who decided long ago that they can't fight anymore.

We are all called to be warriors and winners. But Tony Miller teaches us in this book that it is not enough to *want* success. We must also be willing to embrace *God's process* that will make us successful.

If we learn to embrace that holy process, then we will enjoy the journey to significance.

—J. LEE GRADY, EDITOR, *CHARISMA* MAGAZINE

chapter one

The Journey Begins

M y family and I have had the privilege of living in Clewiston, Florida, for a considerable part of our ministerial life. While that has been a plan divinely orchestrated, it has also been a real advantage because it is an established but little-known fact that Clewiston, Florida, is the geographical center of the world. You can start from there and go anywhere in the world— and the maximum distance would not be more than approximately twelve thousand miles! I have learned that I can go from where I am to anywhere I want to go! The journey begins in me.

1

Lift your eyes now and look *from the place where you are*—northward, southward, eastward, and westward; for all the land which you see I give to you and your descendants forever.

—GENESIS 13:14–15, EMPHASIS ADDED

I HAVE LEARNED THAT I CAN GO FROM WHERE I AM TO ANYWHERE I WANT TO GO! THE JOURNEY BEGINS IN ME.

You too are fortunate, because regardless of where you are, you are at the center of the world. If you are willing to look beyond the obvious and to see the potential that lies within your heart, you can arrive at much more than just a geographical location. You can begin to see your destiny from where you are standing!

To be fair, I must tell you that any journey can be demanding. It is not always an easy trip. There will be hills and valleys, curvy roads, temporary delays and frequent maintenance required. However, if you will supply the desire, the information you hold in your hand will help you with the directions. Though the trip is not easy, it is exhilarating! The views are spectacular, and the rewards are out of this world! It is even more inspiring to consider what you will become along the way.

Anybody Can Do It

The journey is not about how much education you have, what neighborhood you grew up in or who your parents are—it is about you and what you are willing to do that counts. A majority of all the millionaires in America are first-generation millionaires. Many of the most prominent world-class leaders were raised in poverty, were abused as children or have battled with some type of serious disability. When your determination to get up and go forward is stronger than your fear of failure or the nagging obstacles that seek to hinder your trip, your adventure toward significance will begin.

My intention is not to try and convince you to be the best in the world at what you do. That would be quite frustrating, and possibly even debilitating to your confidence. There can only be one person who is the best in the world at what you do. But I am extending an invitation to you to make a commitment to become the best you can be. Learn to recognize—and to maximize—your gifts, talents and opportunities. If you do, your life will be both satisfying and awesome.

Many people who are intent on fulfilling the plan that God has for their lives will have important questions to ask, including the following:

- Is significance a destination, or is it a journey?
- Can you be young and arrive, or must you be old?
- Is significance measured by popularity, wealth, fame or prestige?
- Is a single mother with a limited education, who demonstrates her love for her children by working two jobs to clothe, feed and educate them in order to give them a chance to succeed in life, considered significant?
- Can that place be arrived at alone?

There are more questions that could be asked about finding significance than most anyone could answer. Some people believe that the circumstances of their lives have sentenced them to "second-string status," never to rise to a place of valuable contribution. Others habitually "second-guess" every opportunity and compliment to determine if it's valid.

I want you to hear another voice...one that seeks to call you from the shadows and into the sunlight of hope. You are important to God, and your life is full of God-designed possibilities!

Every journey begins with a step. You may have the ability of traveling ten thousand miles, but you won't leave your room if you aren't willing to take the first step. Getting started is what causes us so much difficulty. It has been my observation that throughout the world, in every walk of life, the men and women who reach a place of influence and impact in their generation have a passion to become what God created them to be. *The focus of our passion is a key to beginning the journey!*

YOUR LIFE IS FULL OF GOD-DESIGNED POSSIBILITIES!

Alfred Lord Tennyson said, "The happiness of a man in this life does not consist in the absence but in the mastery of his passions." Benjamin Franklin once said, "He is a governor that governs his passions, and he is a servant that serves them."

Why do some people succeed where other people have failed? Why are some able to achieve more with less resources than others with greater assets? Why do some accomplish more in a single year than others do in a life-time? It certainly is not a matter of intelligence, education, giftedness or even training. Could the deciding difference be passion?

What would make Lance Armstrong battle cancer and then tackle the stress of the Tour de France on a bicycle, conquering mountain roads and adverse conditions, put-ting his body through rigorous physical exercises in order to win? It was his passion for victory! Why is Michael Jordan known as one of the greatest last-shot basketball players in the history of the NBA? Because of his intense desire to win! What could cause the apostle Paul to go to prison in Rome joyfully, even though he knew that death would probably be the final destination of his trip? It was his passion to take the gospel to Rome and the household of Caesar!

When you see an individual who fails time after time and is unmoved by his lack of progress, you can be sure that the fire has gone out inside. Passion has left! Apathy has begun.

There is a major difference between *having a passion* for something and *being obsessed* with something. Passion is positive, controllable and energizing. It is more than mere human fervor or emotional hype. It is borne by the inter-nal flames of desire and vision. It's like fire in your belly. On the other hand, an obsession is negative and destruc-tive. Obsessions are born of cravings, fear or greed. People with passion become winners at life, while those who are obsessed become workaholics and grumpy! Passion is hard to define, important to maintain and impossible to fake for an extended length of time.

I am convinced that there are seeds of greatness in the heart of every human being God created. There is a divine purpose that no one else can fulfill. Many of those seeds, like sleeping giants, lie dormant inside your heart at this moment. Once awakened, they will move you to a dimension of grace and possibility you have never experienced.

"YOU DON'T HAVE TO BE GREAT TO START, BUT YOU HAVE TO START TO BE GREAT."

There is a strong conviction in my heart that passion—like courage—is transferable. Sometimes it is easier *caught* than *taught*. When we are surrounded by people with zeal for the truth and an eagerness to become all God wants them to be, our lives will be changed. Hope comes alive in the presence of real expectancy!

> I would have lost heart, unless I had believed
> That I would see the goodness of the LORD
> In the land of the living.
>
> —PSALM 27:13

Life will often try to convince you that you face a "hopeless situation." In reality, there are few hopeless situations! Instead, there are people who *lose hope* in the midst of the situations they face. So often we tend to calculate carefully all the costs and become overly cerebral regarding our response to God's invitation to live life abundantly. In doing so, we forget the excitement that comes from taking our first step out of the boat to walk on water.

How the Journey Begins

Are you wondering how to get your journey to significance started? There are several principles that can help you.

1. Make the commitment to get started.

I have heard it said, "You don't have to be great to start, but you have to start to be great." Your greatest challenge is in getting started!

Commitment is essential for accomplishment in life. Committed lives have meaning, purpose and excitement. Tentative living is never satisfying and usually gives way to negativity, critical attitudes and cynicism. Sure, there are times when we are confronted with our humanity, the realization that we are *dressed in flesh*, and all we want to do is sit around and vegetate—doing nothing but wasting time and energy. But tentative, distracted lives are never victorious!

> Indolence wants it all and gets nothing;
>> the energetic have something to show for their
>> lives.
>> —PROVERBS 13:4, THE MESSAGE

> He who tills his land will have plenty of food.
>> —PROVERBS 28:19, NAS

God has so arranged the order of our world that our bread comes by the "sweat of our brow," indicating that there is no promise of success or abundance without the willingness to work for it. (See Genesis 3:17–19.) For what are you saving your energy and ingenuity? Who wants to end a journey with reserve gas still in their gas tank? Why would you want to cease on your journey to significance

with reserve potential still buried within you? Get started!
The difference between the masterful and the mediocre is a
focused effort. God plan is always...start now!

2. Refuse to chase fantasies.

> The one who chases fantasies will have his fill of
> poverty.
>
> —PROVERBS 28:19, NIV

> Work your garden—you'll end up with plenty
>   food;
>   play and party—you'll end up with an empty
>   plate.
>
> —PROVERBS 28:19, THE MESSAGE

A man once gave me this good advice: "If is seems too
good to be true, it probably is!" You cannot live your life
pursuing fantasies that are based on unrealistic expectations and call them dreams. Those types of dreams are as
unreal as the hallucination of someone on drugs! Talking
about success...dreaming about success...waiting for success...while continuing to sit and do nothing is like waiting
for the proverbial ship to come in. Someone once said,
"With my luck, when my ship comes in, I'll probably be at
the airport!"

You are caught up in a mirage when you think you
can get great results from little effort. Those who are
willing to do only the minimum will never make a major
contribution to their generation.

Unless we are willing to enroll in the School of
Preparation, we will never graduate to new levels of significance. What biography or history story have you ever
read of a person who lived in Fantasyland and became a

great hero? Often we look at people who have arrived at a place of success and believe they were *overnight successes*. There are no overnight success stories. We must realize that while successful people were still unknown, they were being faithful, prioritizing their lives to their dreams and calling, focusing on the goals that were before them, celebrating each small victory with gratitude and enduring each setback with grace! They may have become suddenly known, but they were not overnight successes. Fame can come in a moment, but greatness is the result of longevity! Fantasy chasers never stay the course long enough to experience its rewards.

3. Set goals for your life.

Your path to fulfillment is carved by your dreams and forged by your determination. What propels you along are the goals that you set along the way. They become the steppingstones on your path, the markers of the next step in your journey. By setting goals you are able to steer your course like the sail of a ship rather than simply drifting along and letting life happen.

Goals give you the ability to judge your progress in life. Their importance becomes obvious when you understand this: If it cannot be *measured*, it cannot be *managed*. We all have visions of what we want to accomplish and what we want to attain. What transforms those visions into reality is the willingness to formulate them into tangible goals.

It would surprise you to know how many people there are who never focus on a goal. They live their lives haphazardly, expending energy in multiple directions, never realizing how forceful they can be when they totally commit themselves to a cause. The apostle Paul's life was so impacting because his testimony became: "This one thing I do..." (Phil. 3:13, KJV). For most of us, rather than "this one thing I *do*," it is "these forty things I *dabble* in!" Focus is a key to finding good success. The more focused you become, the greater your mastery of abilities and the greater your possibility for accomplishment.

FAME CAN COME IN A MOMENT, BUT GREATNESS IS THE RESULT OF LONGEVITY!

Here is some vital information concerning goal setting:

🌳 Set goals in accordance with your purpose and not just your talent.

🌳 There is a difference between *purpose* and *talent*. You may have a multiplicity of talents, but if the Holy Spirit gives no direction in that area, you will not be effective. We are "called according to His purpose" (Rom. 8:28). If you set all your goals in life based only on what you are talented to do, you may end up following your talent into what is comfortable for you, but not what has been appointed for you.

🌳 God will surely use your talents and gifts. But talent can become blinding and cause you to pursue all the opportunities available to you at the expense of the plan God has for you. How often have we watched as people followed the path their talent took them, rather than focusing on the development of their talent as it relates to the purpose of God for their lives.

🌳 Make small, incremental goals so you can see progress.

🌳 Don't fall into the trap of setting only life-term goals. It can become overwhelming. Make short-term goals (one week to twelve months), mid-term goals (one to three years), long-term goals (three to five years) and lifetime goals. Set goals for your family, your finances, your health, your ministry and your career. Don't think in terms of just one area of your life. Your journey is not just about one aspect of your life, but rather your life as a whole.

🌳 Write down your dreams, and then memorize them.

🌳 Habakkuk 2:2–3 says, "Write the vision and make it plain on tablets, that he may run who reads it. For the vision is yet for an appointed time." The instructions by the Lord to the prophet Habakkuk refers to a common practice in his day of writing public notices with large characters on clay tablets so those walking by or running by could read the message. Once they read it they could respond accordingly.

🌳 When you take the time to write out what you are dreaming about, you create an avenue for inspiration and focus. The old adage says, "Plan your work, then work your plan."

🌳 Once your goals have been written, take the time to move them from the place where they are written to the chambers of your heart. It is only when our plans become more than a "to

do" list that we begin to enjoy the journey.
Life is lived from the inside out, and dreams
really do become reality!

🌳 Planning can be quite burdensome! I often
seem to grow impatient with the planning sessions I am forced to participate in. For some
reason it seems to take the spontaneity out of
life. It is tedious to move my thoughts toward
paper and allow them to be analyzed. See,
anyone can get carried away in the round-
tables of conversation, but when you are
required to *write your detailed plans on paper*,
details arise that were previously unseen.
Problems . . . obstacles . . . weaknesses . . .
required resources, they all become obvious.

🌳 Be sure your progress is measurable.

🌳 You must be able to mark the outcome of the
goal in some fashion. If you can't measure it,
progress will not be easily detected and frustration can become a roadblock.

4. Pursue the wisdom needed to complete the journey.

Ignorance is deadly. Proverbs 4:7 says, "Wisdom is the
principal thing; therefore get wisdom. And in all your getting, get understanding." If we are going to get started and
sustain our joy in the journey, wisdom will be needed. Our
pursuit of wisdom says much about our desire to succeed.

Wisdom comes into our lives through two primary
ways—through mentors or through our own mistakes.
Learning from others is less painful than learning from
our own fumbling through life.

He who walks with wise men will be wise, but the companion of fools will be destroyed.

—PROVERBS 13:20

Our pursuit of wisdom must be consistent and fervent. If we only reach for it when it is convenient, then we will leave our future in the hands of our circumstances, trusting events or other people to produce significance in our lives.

Do not become intimidated by those who know more than you do or who have walked where you are headed. They are a source of information that can help you reach the next place in your life.

One of the things I have noticed in people who desire wisdom to make advancements in life is their inability to draw from the wells of wisdom in the hearts of those who have gone before them. Many times we need the wisdom they could impart to us, but we do not know how to draw out their wisdom. The primary key is to ask questions!

Jesus was a master at helping people make self-discoveries. He did it by asking thought-provoking questions. In fact, He would often answer a question with a question. By asking questions we can tap into the passion in an individual's life and receive an abundance of the resources and knowledge within that person.

5. In every step, stay flexible.

Life is not as structured as we sometimes want to make it. Planning is necessary, you must have a determined focus, and your relationships need to be ordered. But what do you do with the unexpected?

Do you have complete control over your destiny, or does God have some part to play? That question is as old as the theological arguments about the sovereignty of God vs.

the free will of man. But our questions about destiny are not theological debates. This book is meant to help you to navigate successfully the events of life—both seen and unseen—in order to arrive at a place of hearing, "Well done."

I grew up in a pretty normal home. My parents loved each other and me as their only child. They, along with my grandparents, were very involved in my life. My father was a rock; his very presence provided a wonderful sense of security. In my mind, he could do anything! We were, and still are, great friends!

But in our family, my grandfather was the pillar. He was a quiet, unassuming man, small in physical stature, but huge in life! His integrity was known throughout our city, and his love for people made him a friend to everyone. I honestly do not know of anyone who disliked him. He and I were close.

After finishing my first year in college, I was ready to draw from him all the wisdom I could as we worked together for the summer. He loved God so vibrantly. But one Thursday night, with no previous warning signs, my grandfather became extremely ill. My father rushed to my grandparent's home to be with my grandmother as the ambulance came to transport my grandfather to the hospital. As the EMTs were preparing to bring my grandfather from his bedroom, he stopped them. Looking at my grandmother to whom he had been married for fifty-three years, he said to her, "I love you." He then turned to my father and his brother and said, "I'm going now. I expect to see you both in heaven."

My father said, "Daddy, everything will be fine. They

are just going to take you for some testing." My grandfather just smiled. They had been making plans for the business they shared together and the summer vacation times that were coming up. When my dad returned home, he did not say much about the situation, only that we should pray for Granddad.

The next morning we went on to work as usual. However, when I saw my mother turn into the parking lot of the business that my family owned, I knew something had happened. My mother, through her tears, announced to my father and me that my grandfather had died. In that instance my world began to change. He was my hero, my mentor, my vacation partner, my example…and now he was gone. I didn't even have a chance to say good-bye!

WHEN DIFFICULTIES ARISE THAT CHALLENGE YOUR COURAGE TO CARRY ON, BE FLEXIBLE ENOUGH TO CHANGE YOUR DIRECTION.

When life takes a sudden turn, how do you respond? Do you forfeit the destiny God has for you simply because you don't understand the events that have taken place? Is anger your response because you could not be in control?

The Wisdom book gives us strong counsel when it says:

> We plan the way we want to live,
>   but only GOD makes us able to live it.
> —PROVERBS 16:9, THE MESSAGE

Every day I am held together by the truth of the psalmist: "My times are in Your hand" (Ps. 31:15). It is

impossible for us to "do life" on our own. We must stay
flexible enough to receive His grace for each moment of
life—those we prepared for and those we didn't. We need
His grace in both the seasons of sunshine and in the rain.

Life will always present us broken places, places of pain
and struggle. If your journey has been put on hold, hang
on! Stay on the line until the promise gets back to you.
Wouldn't it be awful to come to the end of life and realize
that the dream that you gave up on was not denied, only
delayed?

When difficulties arise that challenge your courage to
carry on, don't change your decision to pursue your potential. Be flexible enough to change your direction. It may be
that another pathway is needed.

Let's Get Started

He who has begun a good work in you...

—PHILIPPIANS 1:6

With a twinkle in your eye and a melody in your heart,
you should begin the course that He has laid out for you.
Look inside and see all the seeds of potential and greatness
that God has entrusted to you. Who knows what God has
planted in you? Celebrate your beginnings! Like Moses,
you must mark your starting places (Num. 33:1–2). When
you clearly define your starting places, you will be able to
encourage yourself throughout the journey. When
discouragement comes, all you will have to do is look back
at where you came from to find a cause for rejoicing! Look
what the Lord has done!

Are you ready for the word of the Lord in your life to
come to pass? You are about to step into the greatest days

of your life, days filled with purpose and passion. As Bishop T. D. Jakes would say, "Get ready; get ready; get ready!"

It's time for your journey to begin. The road to significance is waiting for you.

chapter two

"Come Up Here"

D o you ever find yourself asking the question, "Is there more to life than what I am living? Is this all there really is?" If so, this could be the beginning of the greatest day in your life. Allow the sense of "divine dissatisfaction" that you are feeling to work on your behalf to shake you from status quo living. Step out of your comfort zones into a life of significance.

There is one common law to life: No one gets to choose *how they were born*, but everyone gets to choose *how they will live*. You didn't get to choose your skin color, the family you were born into or your financial status, but you do get an opportunity to take what has been given to you and create a new world!

John Johnson, one of the wealthiest men in America, once said, "Men and women are limited, not by the place of their birth, not by the color of their skin, but by the size of their hope."[1] Hope is what gives us the expectation of something good happening in our lives. It allows us to experience a whole new perspective in life.

ALLOW THE SENSE OF "DIVINE DISSATISFACTION" THAT YOU ARE FEELING TO WORK ON YOUR BEHALF TO SHAKE YOU FROM STATUS QUO LIVING.

"Man, it looks so different!" Those were the words I used to describe the feelings and thoughts that were filling my mind as I looked out from the window of the Delta Airlines Boeing 767 in which I was flying. I was traveling from my home in south Florida to the West Coast. The Rocky Mountains below were just one more part of the spectacular, ever-changing landscape that had been so beautiful that day. That day, as I looked from my window seat at the awesomeness of God's creative ability, I learned a valuable lesson. It suddenly became apparent to me that *perspective* is paramount to understanding our world!

Traveling has been a part of our family tradition since I was a young child. Every summer was spent sightseeing and visiting some of the historical landmarks of our nation. During my teen years, my father would often drive us on our family vacations, providing us opportunity for "road time" as we roamed the hills, mountains and countryside of our great nation. The beauty and wonder of creation were awesome to behold. We saw the vastness of the plains, the magnificent might of the mountain ranges and the seemingly endless miles of agriculture.

I remember so clearly the first time we were able to travel by car to the Rocky Mountains. As we approached them from a great distance away, they stood tall…majestic…immovable. They seemed impossible to cross. The nearer we got to them, the more imposing they became. It was so obvious that in their grandeur they also had the ability to obstruct progress and limit vision. As a teenager I would close my eyes and imagine what the explorers and pioneers who helped settle that region must have gone through in their efforts to build homes, establish towns and eventually construct highways in that region of our nation and then on beyond to the West Coast. It seemed impossible!

However, that day in the plane something changed. It wasn't the mountains and their imposing landscape, nor was it the remarkable ingenuity it would take to tame them. What changed was *my perspective*! As we began our flight pattern over those same mountains, they appeared to become as ripples on a small pond. The higher we went, the less imposing they appeared!

Everything has to be judged in its proper *context*! When a man says we are $30,000 in the red, it may or may not cause panic. If the company was expecting to be $50,000 in the red, then $30,000 is cause for jubilation. However, if they were expecting to be $50,000 in the black, the news of the deficit could be reason for consultation. Our perspective has to have a proper context to become effective in our progress!

Often in our lives there are obstacles and barriers that

appear to be insurmountable. They become revealers of limitations and inadequacies, hindering progress and stifling our pursuit of destiny. In those moments, what we need is a fresh perspective. Our focus must begin to reach beyond the natural and its finite barriers to the supernatural and its infinite power. We need a viewpoint that comes from higher ground!

GOD WANTS US TO SOAR HEAVENWARD TO HIS ETERNAL PERSPECTIVE!

It is my desire to challenge each of you, as people full of divine potential and purpose, to recognize that the call of God to us is always *upward*! God is extending an invitation for us to leave our little world of pettiness and selfishness and come into His great big world. He desires to move us from our limited "peephole" view of life to a place of divine opportunities and unlimited possibilities so that we anticipate each day or week with passion, wonderment and faith. He wants us to soar heavenward to His eternal perspective!

Get ready, now, my friends, for God is about to take you to new arenas of faith in this threshold of the twenty-first century. It may require that past ideologies and habits are left below in order to embark on your journey to significance. Every new adventure requires a willingness to leave our comfort zone and pursue new truth that can elevate us to higher levels.

Get Ready for Your Journey

Each new dream or vision that you have in your life will require a willingness on your part to obtain the wisdom and thinking to possess it. Personal growth is a mandate if your journey is to be fulfilling.

There is a consistent pattern throughout the Bible of what happens in a life that God chooses to use and improve.

The call

First, there is a *call* that goes forth. God invites ordinary people to engage in acts of extraordinary trust. He calls you to break your natural tendency to make excuses, magnify limitations and discredit your abilities. By their obedience, the people who answer His call secure their destinies and fulfill God's purposes.

The fear factor

There is always a *fear factor*. Most of the time God has a habit of asking people to do things that seem to scare them. It may be the fear of inadequacy, like the fear Moses experienced when he exclaimed, "O my Lord, I am not eloquent...I am slow of speech and slow of tongue" (Exod. 4:10). Perhaps it is the fear of failure holding you back as it held back the ten spies viewing Canaan who said, "We saw the giants...and we were like grasshoppers in our own sight, and so we were in their sight" (Num. 13:33).

The fear factor has to be confronted and overcome. I used to think that God would never ask someone to do something he could not do or was afraid to attempt. Then I read the Bible. I was amazed to discover that Jesus was constantly asking, or inviting, people to do things they "could not do." He asked a man with a withered hand to "stretch out your hand" (Matt. 12:13). He told a dead man to come to Him: "Lazarus, come forth!" (John 11:43). Withered hands don't stretch and dead men don't walk, but both did so at His command.

Make the decision

The third factor that is a part of the pattern in Scripture is that a *decision is always required.* Sometimes, as with Moses, people say *yes* to the invitation and change history. At other times, as in the case of the ten spies, people say *no* and make history. But people always have to make a decision concerning their destinies.

PERSONAL GROWTH IS A MANDATE IF YOUR JOURNEY IS TO BE FULFILLING.

Abraham found that to be true when he took his son Isaac to the mountain in obedience to God's request for a sacrifice. Covenant truths that could not be discovered in the confines of his present location were revealed "in the Mount of the LORD" (Gen. 22:14). Abraham had to leave behind his home, family and servants and go on with just his boy. But as he did, Abraham learned that God's provision and faithfulness are revealed in a place of worship— but at a higher dimension. Abraham was not a novice or even a first-time seeker; he was an experienced faith walker. Yet, the call came to him to "go to...one of the mountains of which I shall tell you" (Gen. 22:2).

The Upward Call

There was yet another occasion when "the LORD called Moses to the top of the mountain, and Moses went up" (Exod. 19:20). Moses received two very important things from God during those forty days on the mountain. He received the tablets of stone revealing the Law of God with His commandments to mankind, and he received the pattern for the construction of the tabernacle in the wilderness. The Law became the foundation for faith and covenant. The pattern for the tabernacle carried the instructions for the establishment of a place of worship where God's presence would dwell with His people.

Every time we choose to go higher, we will find that our faith is strengthened and more completely established and our worship experiences are transformed in their focus and intensity.

All throughout the history of the Old Testament, during their annual journey to Jerusalem for the Passover feast, the children of Israel would sing songs. Those songs are recorded in the Psalms and are known as the *Songs of Ascent* (Psalms 120–134). Each psalm discloses an aspect of the people's heart cry during their journey:

> I will lift up my eyes to the hills—
> From whence comes my help?
> My help comes from the LORD,
> Who made heaven and earth.
> —PSALM 121:1–2

As they began their journey in the lowlands surrounding the city of Jerusalem, the worshipers fixed their gaze toward the city set on a hill, the City of God. It became a beacon of hope and motivation as they made the effort to come before the Lord.

The prophetic voices of the Old Covenant continually point us upward. The following will show some examples of this upward call:

- Jerusalem was pictured as Zion, the Old Testament picture of the triumphant church (Ps. 48:1–2; 50:2; Heb. 12:23–24).

- The saints would rule and reign with Christ in Zion as they were lifted above all the other "hills" to become the chief mountain in the earth (Mic. 4:1–2).

- In the Scriptures, mountains and hills are prophetic metaphoric pictures of kingdoms, whether man ruled or God ruled.

- The prophet Micah recognized that the day would come when people would no longer be gathered to the man-directed and humanly sustained "kingdoms" of our own making. Instead, they would join the throngs of people who are hearing the call to a higher place—the kingdom of God and the house of the Lord (Mic. 4).

Sometimes all we need is a word of encouragement to change our perspective. Words often are the instrument that God uses to plant dreams and hope in our hearts. That is why words that are fitly spoken bring tremendous blessing.

The prophet Jeremiah brought a word of direction to a congregation that was about to base their hope of future success on fantasy. Previously, a prophet had declared that the captivity of Judah would be ended in two short years. (See Jeremiah 28.) It would be hard, but they could endure. Two years is long, but not unbearable. Everyone shouted, "Amen," and then headed home.

GOD ALWAYS HAS ANOTHER PERSPECTIVE ON YOUR CIRCUMSTANCE THAT WILL POSITION YOU TO OVERCOME!

As they were leaving for their homes, a prophetic word came to Jeremiah, and he began to prophesy. The word that came from him was that the captivity would not last two years, *but seventy years*. What a minute! There is a vast difference between two years and seventy years. However, Jeremiah did not leave the people hopeless or without a strategic plan. His prophetic word included these words:

> Build houses...plant gardens...Take wives... beget sons and daughters...seek the peace of the city where I have caused you to be carried away captive, and pray to the LORD for it; for in its peace you shall have peace...Do not let your prophets and your diviners who are in your midst deceive you... I know the thoughts that I think toward you, says the LORD, thoughts of peace and not of evil, to give you a future and a hope.
>
> —JEREMIAH 29:5–11

God always has another perspective on your circumstance that will position you to overcome! That day He gave the children of Israel a different perspective.

Called to Rule and Reign—in This Life

We who are born again have the promise of ruling and reigning in life with Jesus Christ (Rom. 5:17). We are destined to win, not only in eternity, but also in *this* life! In order for that to become actualized in our everyday living, our perspective must change. Far too many people are talking about the "ideal." They proclaim their authority as believers and act as though they don't have a care in the world. However, in reality they are living far below the standard of living that Jesus gave His life to purchase. Instead of being victorious and abounding, their lives have become a series of disappointments, compromises and confused endeavors. They know what it means to be "in church" or "in trouble," but they never received the information they needed to realize who they are *"in Christ"*! When viewed from the latter, life looks much different.

Undaunted Courage is Stephen Ambrose's best-selling account of the Lewis and Clark expedition. After two years of battling nearly insurmountable problems— hunger, fatigue, desertion, hostile enemies, severe illness and death—the party had reached the headwaters of the Missouri River. All their advance information had led them to believe that once they reached the Continental Divide, they would face about a half-day journey, and then reach the waters of the Columbia River and float safely to the Pacific Ocean. They were on their way to hero status. The hard part was behind them. Or so they thought.

Meriwether Lewis left the exploring party behind to climb the bluffs that were just ahead of them, enabling him to see the other side. He was hoping to see the waters that would carry them the rest of the way, but what he got was a new perspective. Rather than seeing sloping valleys and easy trails, Lewis became the first non–Native American to lay eyes on the Rocky Mountains!²

What do you do when you think you are about finished and ready for a breakthrough, and you realize you have really just begun? How do you, as a leader, rally the troops when they are ready for rest, and the next day calls for the most intense effort you have ever given?

That often happens in our lives. We launch out into a new adventure—start a new job, open our own company, take on a new ministry assignment, begin a family. The initial days are filled with hope and excitement. We are on our way to new levels of success, and then suddenly, instead of smooth sailing we are staring at the Rocky Mountains! What happens next?

STRENGTH, WISDOM AND VISION ARE NOT UNATTAINABLE, BUT THEY ARE OFTEN LOST FROM YOUR VIEW IN THE CLOUDED ENVIRONMENT OF LOWLAND LIVING.

Can you image Lewis as he motioned for the other members of his traveling party to stay back for a few minutes while he thought about how to deal with this "new information." No doubt he felt much the same as a father feels when he has to tell his children that the disease attacking their mother has not left, but rather is calling for more radical procedures.

Eventually, crossing the Rocky Mountains would be the greatest achievement of Lewis's and Clark's lives. The challenge would demand enormous creativity and perseverance. It would lead them to spectacular sights and unforgettable memories. It would build confidence in them. But none of that could be seen on *this side of the Rockies!* They would have to view those rewards from a different perspective.

I remember that when my daughters were little girls, they disliked having to stand around with a group of adults and hold my hand. Often they would pull on my arm, attempting to get my attention. When I would look at them, they would raise their little hands toward me, signaling their desire to be lifted up into my arms. One day in particular we were out for a family outing, watching the local annual parade. My daughter Holly did not want to stand amongst the legs of those we were standing with. She began to tug on my arm, very unhappy with her conditions, until I finally picked her up. I realized something that day—my picking her up did not get her any closer to the parade; it only changed her viewpoint.

Strength, wisdom and vision are not unattainable, but they are often lost from your view in the clouded environment of lowland living. If you are to obtain any measure of effectiveness in your lifetime, you must learn to get a new perspective!

It is time to stop living your life pressured by trouble and confused by circumstances. Life may have dealt you a setback. Unexpected conflict may have sapped your spirit, leaving you staggering to find direction and hope. Plans may have gone awry. People you were counting on may have walked away and let you down. The economy may have fallen when your investment counselors told you it was rising.

No "Adversity Exclusion"

John the Revelator experienced such a world. He found hope while living in a world that was chaotic and oppressive. Having been a part of the ministry team during Jesus' years of earthly ministry, he had seen the miracles and heard the teachings. He was present when Jesus fed five thousand with a little boy's lunch. He watched Jesus raise Lazarus from the dead. He questioned Jesus' powerful abilities along with all the other disciples just prior to Jesus calming the storm while they were at sea.

John experienced the loneliness of the Crucifixion, the unequaled joy of visiting the tomb after the Resurrection and the outpouring of the Holy Spirit in the upper room. He was there when Peter preached his first sermon and three thousand people got saved. However, there was one thing John still had to learn: There is no "adversity exclusion" clause in the covenant we have as believers.

Because of his bold faith and uncompromising preaching, persecution and rejection became a way of life for John. Not knowing what to do with John, the leaders of his day banished him to the isle of Patmos as his ultimate punishment, not for doing evil or for disobedience, but rather for obeying the commandment of the Lord—preaching the gospel.

Good people really do experience difficult days!

During such experiences the key is our ability to recognize the *invitation* that comes to us in the midst of every difficulty. When trouble shows up at your door, realize that promotion and increase are being offered. Don't faint, murmur or complain. Go higher!

That's what John did:

> I, John, both your brother and companion in the tribulation and kingdom patience of Jesus Christ...was in the Spirit on the Lord's Day.
>
> —REVELATION 1:9–10

John reached for an internal source that would lift him to a new perspective. He found his place *in the Spirit!* And the results were a fresh revelation of Jesus Christ.

He heard and saw Jesus, not in the grumbling of life, but in the Spirit! You will never find your answers in your complaining. As long as we are determined to murmur, we tie God's hands to help us.

THERE IS NO "ADVERSITY EXCLUSION" CLAUSE IN THE COVENANT WE HAVE AS BELIEVERS.

A murmuring heart says, "I don't believe God will help me because He doesn't care about me!" It is an accusation against the faithfulness of God. Don't murmur...change your location. Get in the Spirit!

Once there, John received revelation about the condition of his world. *Revelation* is the unveiling of things that have been veiled. A revelation is not something you *design*, but rather something you *discover*. It was there...just hidden.

The revelation God has for us has not been hidden *from*

us, but *for* us! Anyone can find the revelation, but not on his or her own terms. Revelation is revealed only to those who conform to God's criteria!

John was the bishop over the churches of Asia Minor. In his revelation, he was first given instructions for the churches of Asia Minor, most of which were in turmoil. But then John was once again invited higher.

> After these things I looked, and behold, a door standing open in heaven. And the first voice which I heard was like a trumpet speaking with me, saying, *"Come up here,* and I will show you things which must take place after this." Immediately I was in the Spirit.
>
> —REVELATION 4:1–2, EMPHASIS ADDED

Once again we see the call to come higher! It would have been easy to become discouraged after receiving the messages given to the churches, which exposed their weaknesses and failures. But God always has a redemptive plan. We just have to know how and where to find God's plan.

Think of how this must have affected John. His heart was bursting with desire and concern for those he had led and influenced, but he was unable to express it due to his confinement on Patmos. Have you ever felt there were situations in life that needed your attention, but you were unable to respond due to some circumstance of life? Or were there times when you felt you had reached your limits of supportiveness, yet it was not enough to salvage the day?

The Spirit of God was letting John know that "after these things" there is still something God will do. After the divorce…after the bankruptcy…after your friends have walked away and wounded your heart through their lies and misrepresentations—after all this, there is still hope! When important issues have become clouded by emotions and finding the will of God seems so hard, come up here!

John moved from the boundaries of human perception to the expanse of heaven's invitation! There was a *door opened*! For most of us it is easy to look for a "door out" of adversity, but for John, the invitation was given with a door open! It was open to God's presence and the throne room of the universe! A throne that was fixed...unshakable...immovable! He had been invited to the place where destinies are forged and purposes are determined.

GOD ALWAYS HAS A REDEMPTIVE PLAN. WE JUST HAVE TO KNOW HOW AND WHERE TO FIND GOD'S PLAN.

At that point, John recognized that Jesus was King! His Word will stand forever. The promise lives because He lives! How could John remain defeated or despondent after such an encounter? How could he feel sorry for himself because of what he had been through? He had made the choice to respond to God's invitation to *live life at a higher dimension*. Because he responded, he was granted the privilege of seeing the majesty and might of Him who is seated on the throne of heaven.

As a result of his readiness to act, he found himself in a worship service in heaven! He had been invited to God's world, and he saw the throne of God and the unshakable Word of God. What else could he do but worship? What else can we do but worship the glory of God?

Make no mistake here. The invitation that was extended to John...to Moses...to David...is now personally being given to every person. *Come up here!* Come with your family issues—come and worship. Bring your business and come. Don't hide your disappointments, your questions and your fears. *Come on up.* Bring your children, too! *Come up higher!*

chapter three

What Are You Hearing?

You are a masterpiece in progress! Inside of your life is miraculous power at work, shaping and defining a person who will be mighty. You are not finished, but you are on your way. The invitation has been extended.

Life is a journey, and every journey has a destination. A true traveler knows where he wants to go and can discern if he is on track to arrive at his destined goal. It can be compared to shooting a bow and arrow. A bull's-eye has been painted on a target, and the archer aims for the target. Everyone wants to hit the bull's-eye in the journey of life! However, in life we often shoot our arrows *first*, and then we paint the bull's-eye around the arrows we shot! That is a formula for wasted time and energy.

Jack Hayford once said, "The secret to being current in the move of God and staying successful is a listening heart." A listening heart is a treasured possession for anyone serious about the journey to significance.

DEATH AND LIFE ARE IN THE POWER OF YOUR TONGUE. YOU CANNOT CONTINUE TO TALK LIKE A BEGGAR AND LIVE IN THE PALACE.

Words create pictures! Every time you hear something said, you visualize those words on the canvas of your mind. That is why it is strategic to be aware of what we hear. Jesus said:

> "If anyone has ears to hear, let him hear." Then He said to them, "Take heed what you hear. With the same measure you use, it will be measured to you; and to you who hear, more will be given."
>
> —MARK 4:23–24

Jesus is instructing His followers that it is important to take care of your hearing. It becomes the key to what we will receive!

It is not unusual for someone to become discouraged with the journey through life and to start allowing negativity to reside within. When that happens to you, you must determine in your heart that regardless of your circumstances or what decisions you may have made in the past, you now refuse to poison your future with the pain of your past. Death and life are in the power of your tongue. You cannot continue to talk like a beggar and live in the palace. You have to adjust your speaking.

One day I was discussing speech dysfunction with a medical doctor. During the conversation, I learned something that changed my life. She explained to me that many children who battle with speech problems do not have vocal problems or even physical problems with the structure of their mouth. Rather they have ear problems! She told me that when a child is brought to her office for speech therapy, the first thing they check is the child's hearing.

Wow! That day it was revealed to me that the reason so many people are negative in their talking and pessimistic in their outlook on life is because they are not hearing properly. You must be careful how you hear! Much as a car radio is full of static when it is not "tuned in" properly, you too can have static and confusion in your walk when your ears are not tuned to hear the voice of God!

Receptivity is the ability to hear and respond. You must be quick to hear and quick to respond if you are to move forward in your life.

Many voices clamor for your attention in the course of every day. Whether they are voices from the place of your employment, the responsibilities of home or the desires of your social life—they are vying for your time and energy. None of them are without significance. They all have some point of entrance into your life. You will have to be able to clear the air and discern the voice that is from God! If you can hear...you can succeed!

After his confrontation with the prophets of Baal in Israel, Elijah became discouraged and ran to a cave to hide. While he was there, fatigued and lonely, the Lord came to him and asked, "What are you doing here, Elijah?" (1 Kings 19:9).

Elijah's response was to remind God of his passion for the things of God. "I have been very zealous for the LORD God of hosts; for the children of Israel have forsaken Your covenant, torn down Your altars, and killed Your prophets with the sword. I alone am left; and they seek to take my life" (v. 10). It seemed to him as if all of his efforts had no lasting results. He was ready to give up.

But God wasn't giving up on Elijah. God invited him to the entrance of the cave.

Suddenly a tornado began to blow through the canyons and mountainsides. Boulders were blown around. Trees were uprooted. No sooner had the tornado passed than the earth beneath him began to shake with an earthquake. The mountain shook as if it were going to fall down flat. Soon it passed. But as soon as the shaking stopped, a thunderstorm the likes of which Elijah had never seen began. Thunder rolled across the earth and lightning danced across the sky. Trees were struck and burst into flames. But soon, the thunderstorm was gone.

As Elijah continued to stand there he began to feel a gentle breeze blowing. In contrast to the ravages of the previous hour, the stillness was audible. Something was different about this breeze. God was speaking in it!

Loved one, it is important that you learn to discern the voice of God. The question is, "What are you hearing?" Some things make a lot of noise and come with a great demonstration, but there is no voice in it for you at that moment. If you allow yourself to be tricked into believing that God only speaks loudly and in raw power, it is possible you will miss the instructions that will change you forever. Guard your ears from the distractions that seek to drown out His gentle voice.

How often have you walked into your house and called for your teenager, only to realize the CD player was turned up so loud your teen could not hear you call? No matter how loudly you screamed, it would be impossible to get your teen's attention over the clamor of that noise. The same is true in your relationship with God. Many times so much of our *stuff* is turned up so loud that when He comes to visit and speak vision to us, we cannot even hear His voice.

Let's discuss a few things that will hinder your ability to hear.

Willingness to Accept Mediocrity

The word *mediocre* comes from a Latin word that means, "to go halfway up the mountain." It denotes something that is done in a halfway manner. Mediocrity is an attitude of the heart.

Too often Christians are satisfied with what they have and do not reach for anything more. *Their contentment becomes a place of containment!*

> The smallness you feel comes from within you. Your lives aren't small, but you're living them in a small way.
>
> —2 CORINTHIANS 6:12, THE MESSAGE

Your satisfaction with status quo becomes a barrier to your listening heart. Rather than being "quick to hear," you become quick to justify your ineffectiveness and spiritualize your barrenness!

God has called you to be exceptional. When you continue to flounder in the land of "Barely Enough," you are robbing God of His investment and yourself of your destiny. God's standard for His creation is excellence. If you accept anything less, you have chosen to live below your privilege as a child of God.

I once saw a man who was an animal trainer for the circus, specializing in training elephants to perform for the huge crowds of people that came. The big animals were mammoth, and I wondered how the trainer was able to train them—or even to confine them. He told us that elephants have a tremendous memory, but they are not necessarily smart. When they are young and weigh just a few hundred pounds, they are tied by one leg to an iron stake that is driven into the ground. They try continually to get free. They pull against the chain hundreds of times, but the stake is strong enough to hold them at that age. Even though they pull and pull, they never go anywhere. Then, as they get older, they stop pulling against it. They have begun to believe they will never break free. When fully grown, one elephant is strong enough to pull down the entire circus tent, but each elephant is held by a small chain and by *the memories of previous days!*

The same is true for many of us. Many people live on Memory Lane, convinced by previous failures or limitations that they can never do anything significant. So they stop pulling!

Maybe someone once said to you, "You can't do that" or "You don't think things through enough to be a leader." Maybe a family member told you, "You aren't smart enough to own your own business." Maybe it was a bank officer who said, "You will never own a home." When those words were spoken, zap! A stake was driven in your mind, and you are still setting your vision by the limiting words of those statements!

STOP LIVING ON MEMORY LANE! IT IS TIME TO HEAR A NEW SONG AND DO A NEW THING!

Friend, God is not intimidated by your limitations! He already knows what they are, why they exist and where they are located. He is big enough to change your weaknesses into strengths. God delights in giving you a dream that is too big for you to do in your own might. He wants you to get excited about His plan for your life and to take the leap of faith that will move you into the awkwardness of knowing, "If God doesn't come through for me, I am finished!"

Pull up the stakes that are holding the chains that keep you content with mediocrity. Stop living on Memory Lane! Stop singing the blues! It is time to hear a new song and do a new thing!

Familiarity

Now He could do no mighty work there, except that He laid His hands on a few sick people and healed them. And He marveled because of their unbelief. Then He went about the villages in a circuit, teaching.

—MARK 6:5–6

Jesus' ministry had begun to explode in popularity. Tremendous signs and wonders were being done in many cities. When Jesus came to His hometown of Nazareth, suddenly the meetings changed. What happened? Didn't Jesus have the same anointing that day in Nazareth as He was demonstrating in other cities? Were there too many strongholds in Nazareth? Wasn't the worship good enough? Didn't they break through into God's presence?

These questions are often the statements of people who use them to explain why nothing miraculous ever happens in their lives or churches. We have become great at explaining away the obvious!

What happened in Nazareth that day is a common barrier to people all over the world. *The people could not get beyond their familiarity!* Jesus was too much of an everyday commodity. They knew His family and His previous place of employment—His life was an open book to them. And because of it, they could not "hear Him"!

Has God ever used one of your closest friends to speak a word of promise to you that could change your life forever, but you were unable to hear it because it came through a familiar vessel? How often has He done this when you were totally unaware of the moment of destiny?

How often have you listened halfheartedly to the message of your pastor, but responded exuberantly when a visiting speaker said the same thing? Or has your spouse told you that she or he has a word from the Lord for you, but you remained complacent about it until a business guru gave you the same idea? Why did that happen? It happened because of familiarity!

It may be familiarity with the place you live. You may have lived in the same city, with the same people, for so long that you no longer expect anything different to happen. At times it is difficult to hear something new and fresh, something that will challenge you to rise to new levels. You may have become very comfortable with "status quo" living. "I've lived here all my life," you say. "That hasn't ever happened here."

Instead of being an instrument of change, have you remained locked up in your everyday cycles of familiarity? Just because you go to work the same way every day, eat at the same restaurants and dine out on the same nights, your entire life does not have to be paralyzed by routine! Develop a conscious hunger to listen for anything new.

Traditions

All too well you reject the commandment of God, that you may keep your tradition...making the word of God of no effect through your tradition...

—MARK 7:9, 13

There is something that is more powerful than the Word of God! I know that may be shocking for you to read, but nonetheless, it is true. In this example from the Book of Mark, Jesus was telling a group of religious teachers that they had invalidated and incapacitated the Scriptures through their traditions!

When we insist on hearing the Word through the "smoke screen" of our own traditional beliefs and viewpoint, we nullify its truth. Tradition affects our hearing.

In the course of twenty-five years of preaching, many times more than three hundred times a year, it has been amazing to me to watch how people receive the Word. I am thankful that many members of the body of Christ are

hungry for truth and desire to know what God is really saying to us. But I have been saddened as I've watched some
people sitting with arms folded and faces snarling as the
truth of the message confronted some traditional belief
system that they held on to. There are some religious
people who will become belligerent over their traditions.

Isn't it amazing that the Pharisees had spent their entire
lives looking for a Messiah, yet when He showed up they
couldn't see or hear Him because He did not come as they
expected Him to come? If that happened to the religious
leaders in Jesus' day, isn't it also likely that there are
churches and individuals today just like that? God intends
to work through these churches and individuals mightily,
molding them into vessels for His purposes and plans. But
their religious formulas continue to get in the way of their
"hearing."

Our world-view is being confronted. Whether it happens over racial issues that have divided our society and
hurt many lives with stereotyping of certain ethnic
groups, or it happens over the involvement of women in
the ministry, tradition is being challenged. Tradition is
robbing some people of relationships and success in life. I
wonder how many people have missed a strategy for victory in the midst of some storm of life simply because it
came through someone of another race or gender? People
who claim to love the Lord, but who hate a man because
of his skin color, are enslaved to the power of traditions
that have no merit.

I once began pastoring at a church that did not believe
that people of color should worship with us. I discovered
that ushers would stand at the doors of the church, speaking in derogatory ways and using racial slurs to try and

drive people of color from our services. I began insisting that the church would be open to whosoever will! It was a hard transition. Threats were made, and some people stomped off angrily. Anonymous letters were even sent to some homes throughout the city, but truth must stand. Tradition—whether social or religious—makes truth invalid. Today our congregation is multiethnic, and our embrace is for everyone who comes!

The challenge for women is still being felt in circles today. Jesus Christ is the only spiritual leader in history who liberates women. Religious tradition always seeks to bind them. Our traditions over music, worship and dress styles all hinder our ability to hear the voice of the Lord and respond creatively and relevantly to our world! Don't allow the power of tradition to keep you from living your life according to the principles found in the Word of God.

Hurts and Offenses

A brother offended is harder to win than a strong city.

—PROVERBS 18:19

Offenses are the brick and mortar we use to build walls around our hearts. When wounds and hurts enter your heart, you begin to shut down your capacity for listening. It then is easy to become preoccupied with who is to blame for those wounds and hurts rather than hearing what is needed to be free.

If you live very long, someone is going to hurt you. That is a reality of life. Jesus said, "It is impossible that no offenses should come" (Luke 17:1). Sometimes an offense is deliberately inflicted upon another person, and at other times they happen accidentally. Either way, your ability to handle them properly will determine your success in having a listening heart.

What about children who become offended at their parents because of some decision the parents made that upset the children's plans? Or a wife who becomes hurt because her husband did not respond in the way she was expecting because he did not know her desires? What about church members who become offended because they were not chosen to lead the committee? By harboring an offense, each of these people has hindered his or her ability to hear.

What do we do? Begin by endeavoring to clear the airwaves. Pursue the one who offended you and seek reconciliation. Don't allow your hurts to drive you inward, causing you to be self-centered and self-protective. God is still at work in your life to bring you to His desired end. Let Him!

Pride

Pride is like bad breath—when you have it no one will tell you that you have it; they just stop coming around. Pride is a killer to the listening heart.

In 2 Kings 5 we are told of a man named Naaman. He was a good man and a man of authority, the commander of a great army. But Naaman had one problem; he was a leper. He was a great man, *but he was a leper*! You may be like Naaman; you may have great qualities...but there is a "but" in your life. No doubt that is true for many people. Often we don't want others to see our "but"!

Naaman wanted to be healed, but there was no remedy for him in his homeland. One day his wife's servant girl told her mistress that she knew of a prophet who could give him a solution if he would listen to him. Because Naaman was such an important person, at first it was hard to receive a word from a servant girl. However, his willingness to humble himself and listen was the beginning of his miracle.

PRIDE IS A KILLER TO THE LISTENING HEART.

Naaman went to visit Elisha. When he arrived, Elisha would not even come out of his house to speak to this great man. It infuriated Naaman. Could not this prophet give him the common courtesy of speaking to him face to face? The issue for Naaman was not just leprosy—it was pride. The word that Elisha sent to Naaman that day was, "Go and wash in the Jordan seven times, and your flesh shall be restored to you, and you shall be clean" (2 Kings 5:10).

That only made Naaman even angrier. Did this man really expect him to get in the muddy, dirty waters of the Jordan River and dip under—not once, but seven times? Naaman turned to go home. His pride and anger were about to rob him of the breakthrough that he so desperately needed. As he prepared to leave, one of his servants spoke to him and said, "If the prophet had asked you a hard thing to do, would you have not done it?"

In Naaman's heart it would have been easier to attempt some impossible task or to pay a large sum of money to obtain his healing. But God's heart was for him to humble himself and be healed. Naaman decided to do what the prophet Elisha said and to obey the word of the Lord. Seven times he went down under that muddy water. Six times he came up a leper, but on the seventh time he was made whole!

Many times God wants us to break through to new places in His kingdom, but our pride hinders us from hearing the simplistic commands that He gives. We are waiting on God to give us some difficult assignment or some impossible task to prove our worth. But all God wants is our obedient response to His voice of invitation.

Maybe God has been asking you to give Him the first thirty minutes of your day. Maybe He wants you to lay down your image and worship Him with passion and expression. It could be that He wants you to honor Him with 10 percent of your resources. Maybe it is to forgive a friend from whom you have been estranged for several years. None of these are difficult challenges, but how often does our pride keep us from hearing them?

What Will a Listening Heart Do for You?

When we are quick to hear and quick to respond, we can expect several things to happen in our lives.

A listening heart will change the atmosphere of our lives.

When Nehemiah stood to read the word of the Lord in Nehemiah 8:5, the people stood to their feet to hear the word. They were ready...expectant! As a result, the atmosphere of the city changed from weeping to one of joy! Nehemiah declared, "The joy of the LORD is your strength" (Neh. 8:10).

Hearing God's voice is a great motivator! His words are "spirit, and they are life" (John 6:63)! The mundane begins to have meaning when you know that you have heard from God. The details and difficulties become worthwhile avenues to a desired end.

A listening heart will open doors for us.

Have you ever seen an employee who was quick to listen to what his employer was saying and then quick to respond with action? What happens to that employee? He gets the promotion. The same will be true in your life.

A listening heart will give us direction.

One of the practical advantages of a listening heart is that it sets the direction for our lives. Once we have direction, we know where we are going. Then decision making becomes much more simplified. If you hear the voice of God telling you what He desires and wants for your life, it becomes much easier to prioritize and focus your energy.

The challenge for you is to maintain your listening heart. What are you hearing? What voices are clamoring for your attention? Make a choice today to keep the soil of your inner man clear of obstacles that would hinder you from receiving God's invitation to a life of significance! You may not clear the roadway all at once, but remember the key is to make progress! When you begin to "tune in," God will respond, and you will hear clearly.

chapter four

Qualified
to Be
Multiplied

E very journey must begin somewhere. Every building
has to have a foundation before it can become an
awe-inspiring edifice. There is no real criticism justi-
fied for those who haven't arrived as long as they are on
their way. Starting points! We all have to have them.

In his book *Can You Stand to Be Blessed?*, Bishop T. D.
Jakes teaches the importance of understanding that the
ability to walk in the blessings of the Lord and our full
potential is tied to our ability to discern the prerequisites
for success.[1] If you do not lay the proper foundation for the
life to which you aspire, you can easily find yourself occupying a place in life that you are unable to maintain. This
is what the secular world has come to know as "The Peter

Principle." The Peter Principle is used to describe people's ability to rise to the highest level of their incompetencies.

Many people have discovered the harsh reality that it is easier to *obtain* than it is to *maintain*. For example, it is much easier to get married than it is to love, encourage and nurture a marital spouse. One only takes moments, the other a lifetime. One comes with a flash of emotion and giggles, while the latter demands focus and commitment, even through the tears.

If our life is going to new levels and places of enlargement, we must step out of the routines of mediocrity. Too often we find ourselves running in circles, ending up at the same place in life, because we are captured in a cycle. The truth is that we are disoriented, confused about where we are and where we need to go.

Recently my wife and I visited a major city in America where we had never been. We—or she, I'm not sure which—decided to go the local mall to do some shopping. We knew of a particular store where we wanted to shop, but we were unsure of its location. As we entered the mall, there in the middle of the aisle was a directory listing all the stores and their locations. There was also a map of the mall, with the floor plan of each level, showing the exact location of the store we wanting to go to. On the map was a large yellow arrow showing the entrance where we had just entered. Next to the arrow were the words, "You are here." The management of that mall knew that we could not find our way to where we were going if we could not locate where we were.

That same fact is true in our lives. Instead of wandering aimlessly through life, hoping we accidentally bump into our destiny, we have to stop and locate ourselves in order to move forward with effectiveness. We cannot treat our purpose in life like a lotto game of chance. Fulfilling your destiny is never a matter of chance, but rather a matter of choice.

It was the ability to choose that separated mankind from all the other creative order. The members of the plant kingdom—trees, shrubs, flowers—do not get to choose their time of blossoming and bearing. They respond to seasons. No matter how much faith is exercised, a maple tree in Maine will lose its leaves in January, and a tulip will not bloom in Wyoming in February.

The members of the animal kingdom do not make destiny choices either. While many animals have been domesticated and trained, the fact remains that, left to themselves, they will respond by their instincts and not by reason.

But man is different. When God made man He put within his DNA the power of volition. He was a walking, talking and thinking reflection of God Himself. God did not make him a robot that would serve by command void of choice, but instead a creative partner that must "will"— make a determined decision—to serve because of desire. As a member of humanity you are not locked into seasons. In fact, you can be fruitful "in season and out of season" (2 Tim. 4:2). Nor are you bound to reactions of instinct only. By God's design you have the power to resist your base nature and to respond to sound judgment. So, therefore, the ability to chose becomes one of your greatest gifts and freedoms.

It is important to note that *the only real freedom we have in life is the freedom to choose.* That freedom should be exercised with wisdom and counsel. For once you choose, you become a captive to your choices.

As you earnestly choose to walk in God's ways, seeking to fulfill His purposes in your life, you will find that He qualifies you for increase and promotion. *No one is born qualified; we become qualified through God's shaping.* It is His processing in your life that enables you not only to obtain, but also to possess your promise without having to forfeit the new territory you take.

That pathway toward greatness begins with what seem to be simple, insignificant decisions. Yet, when lived out over the span of a lifetime, those decisions create a transformed life. The people who continually make decisions based on God's plan become the world shakers and history makers of each generation.

King David began his steps toward greatness in a place of seeming obscurity. David was a Bethlehemite working in a family business—much like the early years of Jesus, who also came from Bethlehem and worked in His father's business.

NO ONE IS BORN QUALIFIED; WE BECOME QUALIFIED THROUGH GOD'S SHAPING.

For both of them, Bethlehem was more than a birthplace. It came to represent the place of beginnings. That is where the dream began...at home, among those who knew them best. Giant killers don't begin as giant killers, but rather as those who, in the midst of their ordinariness, sense the invitation to a life of greater significance.

Bethlehem speaks to us of the ability to be *faithful in natural things!* It is there we learn the foundational truth that faithfulness is always the starting point on God's avenue of promotion.

One of the reasons for stories like David's being in the Bible is so we can locate ourselves. Most of the time the biblical characters that we read about are not being presented to us so much as "role models" but rather as examples of men and women who learned how to deal with and respond to God. They were not perfect people...living perfect lives...enjoying perfect conditions. It was not so much their lifestyles or accomplishments that got God's attention, but rather their hearts.

The God with whom we have a relationship has not chosen to reveal Himself to us only in the celestial context of the heavenlies. He reveals Himself to each of us through the earthy: "on earth as is it is in heaven" (Luke 11:2). The earth dimension—with all its intersections and interruptions—is the context of God's working through our lives. For David, it was shepherding. For Jesus, He "learned obedience by the things which He suffered" while being subject to His parents and their family busi ness (Heb. 5:8).

For you to believe that you can become what God has prophetically declared you to be, you first must be able to recognize that God is present and actively involved in the earthly human dimension of your life right now. He cares about the mundane. That which is taking place at your present address—where you live and work—is God's anvil, shaping and processing you for future significance.

Jesus, who came to reveal God to us, did not just appear on the scene as an *overnight wonder*. His birth was anticipated, predicted, prophesied, promised and prepared during two thousand years of Jewish history. Paul refers to this "purposeful pregnancy" in Galatians 4:4 when he declares, "When the fullness of the time had come, God sent forth His Son." Jesus came in time, on time!

Once He was born into the earth, there was still a *timing* issue before He was manifested as the Messiah. He was born, as prophesied, the seed of a woman! Not full grown, not casting out devils and healing the sick, but as a baby.

Friend, you will not arrive at the place of your purpose until the *fullness of time* has taken place. Recognize that God's beginnings are often small, sometimes as insignificant as a seed. We must first become *qualified*, and then we are *multiplied*.

THAT WHICH IS TAKING PLACE AT YOUR PRESENT ADDRESS— WHERE YOU LIVE AND WORK— IS GOD'S ANVIL, SHAPING AND PROCESSING YOU FOR FUTURE SIGNIFICANCE.

We become qualified by our faithfulness in the mundane and unnoticeable places. Then we are released to multiply and increase through the supernatural.

Like Jesus, David was a prophetic wonder. He appeared to be almost an afterthought in Samuel's diligent search for a replacement to Saul. After meeting each of Jesse's other seven sons, almost casually Samuel asked Jesse, "Are all the young men here?" (1 Sam. 16:11).

David's father answered the bewildered prophet by saying, "There remains yet the youngest..." The word *youngest* in Hebrew is *qatan*. *Qatan* carries the idea of insignificance, of not counting for very much—the family runt. Certainly there were no visions of grandeur in Jesse's heart about David, or thoughts that he might be a genuine candidate for the prestigious job of national leader.

His father's attitude about him was confirmed by the job to which David had been assigned—*tending sheep*. It was possibly the least demanding responsibility on the farm. He could do little damage there if he blew the assignment. It was much like many of our first jobs— newspaper routes, bagging groceries or being a parking lot attendant at our church.

So often we fall into the trap of believing that what we are doing right now has absolutely no part to play in what we have been assigned to do in life, *when in reality our present function is determining our future success.* David was faithful with his father's sheep. When a bear and a lion tried to kill a lamb, he rose to the occasion and slew them. He learned the value of responsibility and of becoming trustworthy. Both are primary ingredients in becoming qualified.

Our society has become so enamored with the hype of fame and the glitz of success that we have forgotten that it is the character of a person that qualifies that person for greatness. Lots of *famous* people are not *great*, including Adolf Hitler, Lee Harvey Oswald, Charles Manson and Bonnie and Clyde. They were all famous, but you would not want your children to follow their example. Edwin Louis Cole said, "Fame comes in a moment, but greatness is seen over a lifetime." How true! Many basketball players have hit the winning shot at the buzzer once in their careers and had their name in the headlines the next morning, only to be forgotten a month later. But Michael Jordan is known as the one of the greatest men ever to play the game of basketball because he hit the winning shot many times while playing over fourteen years in the NBA.

God never commits to *talent* alone; rather, He has chosen to commit to *character*. David had "a heart after God."

During David's years in the pasture keeping his father's sheep, it was not so much the skills that were being shaped that would mark him for greatness, but rather his heart. While skills are certainly important and essential to success, what sets people apart and gives them the ability to change their world is their heart. It is the place where dreams are born!

GOD NEVER COMMITS TO TALENT ALONE; RATHER, HE HAS CHOSEN TO COMMIT TO CHARACTER.

In Luke 16, Jesus describes three areas of life that are evaluated in our movement toward promotion. Each is very practical and earthy, yet profoundly important in our development as people who desire to shape the culture in which we live. Each of these areas serves as revealers of our heart.

Faithful in Little Things

He who is faithful in what is least is faithful also in much; and he who is unjust in what is least is unjust also in much.

—LUKE 16:10

Jesus makes a definitive statement of natural characteristics and spiritual truth. The instruction here is very insightful and conclusive. Faithful in little *will be* faithful in much, and vice versa. What you do in the menial tasks of life are indicators of what you will do with major opportunities.

In the years that God has allowed us to steward various ministries at both local and international levels, this truth has never proven to be wrong. When people fail to handle responsibly what they have in their hands presently, you can be sure they won't handle more of it any better. At the same time, I have watched God work in people whom the world would not have seen as potential leaders. Because they nurtured faithfulness in their hearts, God raised them up to become major leaders to the generation in which they live.

God watches what you do with *little things*. What is your attitude when you are given assignments you view as unimportant? When you are asked to serve as a greeter on Sunday morning, being present thirty minutes before service starts, how do you respond? What do you answer when the stockroom employee is absent and your office manager asks you to stay after hours to help organize inventory?

Years ago when we had just entered the ministry, I was serving at a local church as youth pastor and music director. One Sunday morning when we arrived at the sanctuary the sidewalks were a mess. A wedding had been held at the church the previous evening, and for some reason the cleaning crew forgot to sweep the sidewalks.

As I was preparing for the worship service, our pastor walked into my office with a broom in hand and asked me to sweep the sidewalks. Not wanting to be publicly rebellious,

I took the broom and began to sweep. Standing on that sidewalk I learned a valuable insight about myself. Friend, there is nothing like mundane assignments to reveal hidden flaws in your character. Pride, selfish ambition, personal agendas—they all surface when we are asked to do something that seems below our ability or calling.

That morning I learned that it is possible to be *compliant* and still not be *submissive*. I did the sweeping—I was in compliance. But all the while I was swinging that broom, I was rehearsing the speech I felt should be delivered at the next staff meeting. I rehearsed it over and over. All I could think about was how I needed to let these people know: "I have not walked away from the opportunities I had in life to *sweep sidewalks!* Surely you know that I am anointed and a man of destiny. I have been given a mandate for the nations." Those were the thoughts roaring through my head. Moment by moment I was becoming more and more angry and frustrated.

When you fail to recognize that your present actions are making a way for your future positioning, you get frustrated and angry.

Sometime during the sweeping, I heard God's voice forcefully speak to me. Deep inside I heard, "If you aren't faithful with sweeping, how can I trust you with nations?" That was *not* what I wanted to hear. However, it was the very thing that I needed to hear to be broken of my self-righteous, pompous attitude. The issue that day was not rice on a sidewalk or the awkwardness of sweeping a sidewalk in a suit. The issue was not even whether the pastor had the right to ask me to do such a job. The business of heaven that day was to shape a life so that it could become qualified for future use. Instead of continuing to grumble, I took my broom and walked to a back room where I humbly began to repent before God for my attitude.

"Father," I said, "please forgive me. I want to do whatever my hands find to do with all my heart for You. I recognize that my attitude stinks. I need help."

Then I went back to finish the job of sweeping those sidewalks. Soon the choir members, ushers and Sunday school teachers began to arrive. As each walked by I was wiping away tears, sweeping rice and singing. Several, unable to see my tears, responded, "You sure seem happy today!" Oh, if they only knew.

I wasn't happy with the assignment that I had been given, but I was getting a glimpse of what the assignment was producing in me. Our willingness to be faithful in the little things is the prerequisite for being given bigger things.

Be encouraged. Your present assignment is merely serving as a bridge to a great season in your life. Never despise God's little things. He is a wise master builder, and He has a blueprint already laid out for your life. Your present will benefit you if you learn to "not despise the day of small beginnings." (See Zechariah 4:10.)

OUR WILLINGNESS TO BE FAITHFUL IN THE LITTLE THINGS IS THE PREREQUISITE FOR BEING GIVEN BIGGER THINGS.

Never allow the circumstances you are in to deceive you into believing that God has forgotten you. He hasn't. In fact, He is observing you. Refuse to become bitter at those who you think are hindering your progress by limiting your responsibility. Assess your benefits and commit to personal growth. While others saw David only as a shepherd boy doing a menial task, God was seeing a king in the making.

I have a personal assistant who has traveled with me for several years. He is a multi-gifted, highly anointed young man. When he first started, he came to spend three months with me to be mentored. The challenge of traveling several days a week, the demands of our daily schedule, the work of the ministry, the needs of the people to whom we minister—they all demanded he make an adjustment. He could have done what would have come natural and complained, made excuses and quit, thus forfeiting this place of development and the favor God was desiring to give him.

Instead, he chose to assess his benefits. He recognized that I was paying for airline tickets allowing him to travel all over the world. He was staying in some of the nicest hotels on earth. He was meeting some of God's most wonderful people as we went from city to city, and he was being introduced to leaders in the body of Christ that were of the highest caliber. With all those benefits, it would be foolish for him to fuss about late hours, too many services, taking care of product shipments, caring for laundry needs or having to drive when I am tired. He has been faithful! Because of his willingness to serve in the mundane, now God is opening tremendous doors of opportunity for his own personal ministry. God sees the little things!

Faithfulness in Resources

> If you have not been faithful in the unrighteous mammon, who will commit to your trust the true riches?
>
> —LUKE 16:11

Often we try to separate the secular from the spiritual, the real world from the church. We consider things like our jobs, our time, our relationships and our money as secular. Prayer and Bible reading are a part of the spiritual dimensions of our life.

But it is not that easy to separate. Your life is experienced in many dimensions, but you are, at all times, a spiritual being. So what you do with natural resources becomes an indicator of your spiritual life and maturity.

Jesus knew that how a person handles his *treasure* is a sure sign of where his heart will be (Matt. 6:21). If you are expecting promotion and increase in your life and greater opportunities for significance, you must learn that God is interested in what you do with your resources. How you handle your resources determines how the *true riches* are released to you.

The true riches of the kingdom exceed mere finances. God certainly wants His people to prosper, but there are some things that money cannot buy.

I was once in India for one of our Destiny Crusades. Our normal pattern for these crusades was to host a Pastors and Leaders Conference during the day and to hold open-air evangelistic meetings at night. Tens of thousands of people would gather for the preaching of the Word and a time of special prayer and ministry. Many miracles took place in the services each night.

On this one particular night I had finished preaching and had begun to minister to physical needs. As we prayed, a friend came up and said he had a word of knowledge concerning the healing of bones. We began to speak the name of Jesus over the crowd and to declare healing. Suddenly, from the middle of the crowd, a man began to scream. There was a great commotion among the people.

Out from the midst of the crowd a young man, twenty-three years old (as we were told later), began to run toward the platform, leaping and shouting! The people were laughing and applauding.

A medical doctor from Austria, who was part of the ministry team doing medical clinics each day, came to the platform to tell us that he had seen that young man in the clinic the day before. As he shared his story about seeing the young man in the clinic on the previous day, we realized that this young man had walked on his knees for his entire life, unable to stand because of deformities in his bone structure. That night God completely healed him through the gifts of the Holy Spirit and prayer in the name of Jesus Christ. *That is the true riches of the kingdom!*

A single mother who has a transforming encounter with Jesus Christ and is delivered from a drug addiction that had forced her into a lifestyle of selling her body to support her habit—that is the true riches of the kingdom. Money cannot buy that. Silver and gold could never redeem her. Blind eyes being opened, deaf ears unstopped and crippled feet walking are not hype or emotionalism— they are the riches of the kingdom of God being manifested in the world today.

According to Jesus, these kinds of riches are only

entrusted to people who are willing to steward their resources properly. It involves things like budgeting your money responsibly, tithing to the Lord and paying your bills on time.

For too long the church has been caught up in extremes when it comes to finances. Either we believe that God is impressed with our willingness to live in poverty as a sign of our humility, or we begin to believe that money itself is the root of all evil. We may even buy into the fantasy that the abundance of *stuff* is somehow proof enough that God is pleased with us. We start to equate wealth with strength of faith. We fail to take the time to remember what Jesus taught—a man's life does not consist of the abundance of things that he possesses!

DISCIPLINE IN THE USE OF FINANCES IS ONE OF THE FIRST SIGNS OF BECOMING A TRUE DISCIPLE.

Money is neither good nor evil. It possesses no morality. Its morality can only be seen in the life of its possessor. The same one-hundred-dollar bill can support a drug habit, or it can provide support for a missionary. It can pay for a prostitute, or it can buy your wife a new dress.

Money is an indicator! That is why something as secular as "unrighteous mammon" can be used as a heart revealer. Jesus said, "Where your treasure is, there your heart will be also" (Matt. 6:21).

It is hard to image Jesus releasing world-shaking miracles to people who refuse to allow Him the privilege of directing their natural resources. Why would God want to trust supernatural power to raise the dead to someone whom He cannot trust to give Him 10 percent of next week's paycheck?

As a pastor and leader of an international ministry, long ago I determined that I did not want anyone in leadership around me who did not tithe. *Discipline in the use of finances is one of the first signs of becoming a true disciple.*

Faithful in What Belongs to Another Man

If you have not been faithful in what is another man's, who will give you what is your own?

—LUKE 16:12

In a culture of free enterprise and competition, it is hard for those of us born in the West to really grasp the importance of this principle. The mind-set of our day is, "Watch out for number one!" So many times we end up using people and opportunities for *self-promotion* rather than for *self-development.*

As we move forward on our journey we come to realize that how we deal with what belongs to other people affects our potential.

Joshua had to learn to serve Moses before he could lead the conquest of Canaan. Elisha poured water over Elijah's hands before he carried the double portion anointing.

What are you doing with the things that belong to other people? How are you handling the business affairs of the company for which you work? Are you careless with their inventory or orders? Do you leave work with their equipment in your car without their permission?

Even in the church we must face this issue. Young men and women who desire ministry and want to fulfill dreams are undiscerning of this principle. Their lack of understanding can paralyze their effectiveness for a lifetime. Instead of leading properly by protecting and guarding the sheep that have been entrusted to them as a stewardship by a senior pastor, they use the platform given to them for self-promotion and demonstration of their gifts. They create an atmosphere of competition in the church and leadership team, eventually polarizing the congregation and drawing away their "followers" to a new work.

It is a trap! When you violate what belongs to another man, you set yourself up for trouble, heartache and greater disappointment. God will never put His blessing upon those things that you gain through falsehood, deceitful scheming and manipulation.

When my wife and I began in ministry we served on the staff of a great local church. I had a great deal of respect and honor for the man for whom I worked, and submission to him was not difficult. At the same time, he looked at me as a spiritual son. Trust was an important part of our relationship.

My wife and I were young, inexperienced and in need—financially and socially. Not understanding that our need to prosper and to be accepted created a great vulnerability in our lives, we pursued both. However, the means to both can be dangerous.

During our time there, some people developed a murmuring spirit against the pastor and his leadership. At the same time, these same people seemed to love us. They would bless us with special offerings, have us to their home to eat and make us a part of their lives. They attended whatever ministry functions my wife and I led. They were trying to make us a success—or so I thought.

One night while visiting with them, a comment was made concerning the pastor. I had not heard that from them before and was not aware of what was coming. Then someone said, "Tony, you are a great preacher. You would make a great pastor for a new work." About that time my wife, Kathy, kicked me under the table and asked to speak to me in another room.

As we left the group, she said to me, "Don't you understand what is going on here? Wake up!" Suddenly I was aware that I was being set up. Our adversary, the devil, was about to take advantage of my sincerity and ambition to deceive me into a wrongful position.

CHARACTER IS THE FOUNDATION GOD USES TO DETERMINE THE BOUNDARIES OF OUR INFLUENCE AND TO RELEASE OUR PROPHETIC POTENTIAL.

Let me add a word of caution to all of you who desire to have God use you in a significant way someday. Maybe presently you are serving *under* someone, whether it be in a ministry or in the business world. Learn to recognize the difference between genuine encouragement and sincere compliments that edify you and build you up, and flattery. Flattery differs in its motivation. Flattery seeks to gain approval and entrance by means of admiration, when in fact it is a net for your feet (Prov. 29:5). When people are constantly speaking well of your talents and abilities without any regard for your development, beware!

I realized my integrity was on the line. Would I be *faithful in that which is another man's?*

When we returned to the group, I told them that I understood their concern for the church and for our pastor. I also told them, "I need to leave now, but please be assured that I will let our pastor know as soon as I can speak to him everything that you have mentioned here tonight as a concern. I am sure that he would like to know so that he can take care of it." And I left for home. The next day when I saw the pastor, I told him everything about that meeting. I don't know what happened as a result, but I do know we have never been invited to that house again—which is no problem!

I am grateful that I remained faithful to that man and his ministry so that God could promote me and entrust the stewardship of dreams and ministry to Kathy and me.

Everyone wants to accomplish great things. But in order to reach our fullest potential and have a significant impact, we have to allow God to qualify us for increase.

Character is the foundation God uses to determine the boundaries of our influence and to release our prophetic potential. Our character is seen, not in our perfection or in the unattainable standards the religious community sets for itself, but in our willingness to be accountable for our lives and actions to God. Our cry should be, "Search me, O God, and know my heart!" We are first qualified, and then multiplied!

chapter five

A Bump
in the
Road

Few things are as powerful as the potential unleashed by an individual who knows exactly what he or she was created for. That realization has transformed individuals from a life of aimless wandering to people of impact and influence. When anyone, no matter the age, is awakened to the possibilities that are within from a holy Creator's divine design, only heaven can determine that person's limitations!

Yet, intertwined in that call to significance is the need to find the divine plan—God's order—and our human responsibility.

Respond to God's Invitation

One day while I was praying about some specific promises the Lord had given to Kathy and me through a prophetic utterance, God spoke words to me very clearly, words that have changed my life. I heard Him say, "Your prophecy is not inevitable, but it is an invitation into possibility." Recognizing that God was seeking to communicate a truth to my heart and life, I began a journey of discovery that would bring me, to this awareness: I must *respond* to the invitation extended to me, or my life will never change.

Only God can shape the purpose for our lives, but each of us is granted an opportunity to formulate the avenue through which that purpose will be carried out. Far too often we find ourselves responding to life only after it has hit us in the face. Therefore, instead of making a *faith response* to our circumstances, we wind up giving a *human reaction* to whatever event has seized our attention at that moment. You will never fulfill the divine mandate on your life by continually making choices based on the temporary circumstances of a "survive-the-day" mentality. You must choose based upon revealed direction and purpose for your life—that is the avenue to a transformed life.

John the Baptist was a New Testament prophet and the forerunner of the ministry of Jesus. His declaration, "I am the voice of one crying in the wilderness: make straight the way of the Lord," gives us insight into how this prophetic invitation to a higher dimension is actualized (John 1:23).

John tells us that he, as the spokesman, is not the one giving the invitation, but rather he is the voice of one crying. It is foundational for us to understand that any invitation to greatness must first originate in the heart of God. It is His cry, His desire, that is given voice for each person, inviting that person to rise to the level of potential and possibility for which he or she was created and to fulfill God's designed purpose for that life.

You may feel inadequate or even empty of anything to offer, yet God's cry may have awakened a longing in your heart. He cries out to you in your *wilderness*. God is willing to speak a word in the midst of the barren, unproductive parts of your life, those dry places where you have been wandering about confused, *and He calls you out of that wilderness experience!* His Word will become the *seed* for a life of joy and fruitfulness. Where once the soil of your heart was hardened by disappointment, disillusionment and defeat, now your inner field will be fertile with renewed hope and new dreams. The sound of His voice "shakes the wilderness" (Ps. 29:8).

YOU WILL NEVER FULFILL THE DIVINE MANDATE ON YOUR LIFE BY CONTINUALLY MAKING CHOICES BASED ON THE TEMPORARY CIRCUMSTANCES OF A "SURVIVE-THE-DAY" MENTALITY.

It is His Word that prepares the way of the Lord in our lives. In the midst of your emptiness and futility, God's Word builds a highway for you to progress to a higher dimension of living. That is why *one word from God can forever change your life!*

By asserting that he was only the *voice* of one crying in the wilderness, John was calling our memories back to the prophetic proclamation of Isaiah 40, where the prophet said:

> The voice of one crying in the wilderness:
> "Prepare the way of the LORD;
> Make straight in the desert
> A highway for our God.
> Every valley shall be exalted
> And every mountain and hill brought low;
> The crooked places shall be made straight
> And the rough places smooth;
> The glory of the LORD shall be revealed,
> And all flesh shall see it together;
> For the mouth of the LORD has spoken."
>
> —ISAIAH 40:3–5

According to the insights we gain from John's description of the prophetic proclamation and the affect that word can have, we recognize that God, by His Word, brings order into our destiny. As believers, we can do only what heaven gives us permission to do. John was reminding us that God's prophetic word has given us the permission we need to do the impossible. Once we have God's approval, that same Word from the Lord begins to shape our lives and our pathways to be prepared to possess what He has promised.

His Word first shapes us, and then He releases us to shape our world.

> He sent a man before them—
> Joseph—who was sold as a slave.
> *They hurt his feet with fetters,*

He was laid in irons.
Until the time that his word came to pass,
The word of *the LORD tested him.*
—PSALM 105:17–19, EMPHASIS ADDED

The word of the Lord to Joseph first tested him before it changed the circumstances around him or changed those who knew him. The word *tested* implies that it "found him out...revealed his character." It prioritized and authenticated his dream.

Follow God's Order

Order is one of God's priorities! In God's economy, nothing happens before all the prerequisites have been fulfilled. In the natural order, you cannot be eighteen years old until you have been seventeen years old. Yet, in the church, people want to skip the order and get to the prize. We have to comprehend the truth that learning God's order is part of the journey. God will never be in such a hurry that He bypasses the required process.

There must be within us an awareness of God's strategy, His plan of action, if we are to succeed. Many have asked God for a miracle and missed the response from heaven giving, instead of a miracle, supernatural strategies that, when processed, would result in a miraculous transformation. If we will learn to look for the *ways of the Lord* it will be easier for us to walk in our purpose and fulfill destiny.

David discovered that learning God's order was paramount in fulfilling his dream of bringing the ark back to Zion, God's holy city of Jerusalem. He was excited about the opportunity to return the presence of the Lord to its rightful place of preeminence. (See 2 Samuel 6:1–11; 1 Chronicles 13.)

What a desire...to bring God back to the people. Just like David, we must once again desire His presence to be the prevailing influence over our nation. Like David, we can erect a place of continual worship—His holy temple within each of His people. When David returned the ark of the covenant—the tangible dwelling place of God—to Jerusalem, it had been away from the people for twenty years.

ORDER IS ONE OF GOD'S PRIORITIES!

It is interesting to note that throughout his reign as king, Saul had been content not to seek the return of the ark. He was content to have *position without presence,* believing that his natural ability and charisma were sufficient to lead the people and govern the nation.

But David knew that if one day his dream of leading all of Israel back to greatness was ever to become a reality, he would need God to be *with him.* So David went to the house of the now elderly priest Abinadab, where the ark had been kept since it was returned from the Philistines who had captured it in battle from the sons of Eli. He prepared it for the journey to Zion, back to its place in Jerusalem.

Be Willing to Pursue God's Plan

It is important to establish a key kingdom principle: The evidence of desire in your heart is always manifested in your willingness to pursue. Our willingness to pursue is a revealer of passion. David had a passion for the presence of

God. He had a passion to lead a great nation, to conquer enemies, to restore the place of intimacy. *Passion* has been described as "an intense desire that motivates one to action."

If your dreams are not moving you, they will not move anyone else! The invitation to life at a higher dimension has to affect you, calling you beyond the excuses and limitations of your present environment to a level of conquest and pursuit that refuses to be denied.

It is what men like Nelson Mandela, Martin Luther King Jr. and Jim Elliott experienced in their lives. Having believed they were meant to make their worlds different, they were willing to endure rejection, persecution, imprisonment and even death in order to see their dreams realized. Though they experienced setbacks, the passion for their dreams never died.

King David was passionate about moving the ark back to Zion. His challenge came when he learned the sobering lesson that "zeal without knowledge" can be dangerous (Prov. 19:2). While we must have passion to fuel our faith, we must also have direction and order to materialize that for which our faith is reaching. If we do not discern the road signs that give us directions, we will miss the warnings and discover that there are *bumps* on the highway to glory!

These bumps are places in our thinking and striving that cause us to confront ourselves, reassess the process and find "due order." Rather than quitting when things do not turn out as we expected, or becoming frustrated at God and people, we must seek the Lord for instruction. That is what David had to do.

As the processional began from Abinadab's house, there was great celebration and excitement. The king and his companions were full of life and sincerity in their effort to restore the divine and move Israel toward greatness. But *sincerity alone is never enough*. It is possible to be sincere, and to be sincerely wrong! Dancing...music... crowds...none of these are ever enough to cover up our inefficiency in finding God's order.

THERE ARE BUMPS ON THE HIGHWAY TO GLORY!

Forgetting to find God's order opened the door for one the most disappointing days in David's life. A friend was about to die. Uzzah was one of the sons of Abinadab. He had spent his life growing up around the ark. As an assistant to his father in the priestly duties, it is conceivable that he had helped in the daily care of this precious treasure. He was close enough to have become *familiar* with the ark!

As the procession left the house for the city, everyone was overjoyed. They were on the move. Celebration! Joy in the camp! The ark was moving. How often in our lives have we misinterpreted *movement* for *direction*, only to find out later that we were moving in futility or, at best, going in circles? Void of order, we were happy to be going anywhere, only to be awakened suddenly to the reality that our journey had been interrupted. New plans would have to be formulated.

As they prepared to leave Abinadab's house, the choice was made to place the ark on a new cart in order to carry it to Jerusalem. The use of a cart drawn by oxen was not new. The Philistines had sent the ark back to Israel on a cart (1 Sam. 6:1–12).

It is easy to understand that a well-designed oxcart is

obviously a more efficient way of moving an ark than to have it carried by plodding Levites. After all, Levites walking and carrying that heavy load was old-fashioned...out of date. This was a new day—the day of the *new and improved*.

In reality, it was the day that the people of promise copied the ways of their enemies to accomplish their dreams. No one stopped to ask, "How would God want us to do this?" We must realize that we can never embrace methods and techniques without regarding God! We must always ask first, "What is God's order here?"

I tend to believe that David was not being rebellious to God's pattern. It does not appear that he willfully disregarded God's commands in order to "do things my way." However, it does appear that, like many of us, David was caught up in the moment, and he missed a vital principle of every journey—"How do we get there?" Many times it is the journey itself that God is using to teach us dependency, divine order and trust.

There are usually two reasons why people miss God's due order. One is *presumption*. We assume that because we are God's people, we can move ahead without God's plan and somehow accomplish God's purpose. The other is *ignorance*. Both have to do with our willingness to prepare properly. Without proper preparation, we move ahead, venturing toward our promise without the strategy to accomplish our desire. No one can tell at first. Our energy covers our lack of enlightenment.

Everything was wonderful in the procession to return the ark to Jerusalem until they came to the threshing floor of Nacon. At that point the oxen almost stumbled and fell. As the oxen were getting their footing, the ark began

to slide off the cart. Uzzah, the son of Abinadab, reached up to *steady the ark*, for it was about to fall to the ground.
    The Bible tells us this:

> When they came to the threshing floor of Nacon, Uzzah reached out toward the ark of God and took hold of it, for the oxen nearly upset it. And the anger of the LORD burned against Uzzah, and God struck him down there for his irreverence; and he died there by the ark of God.
>
> —2 SAMUEL 6:6–7, NAS

Death! How could that happen? Is God that touchy? No. He is that holy!

The parade was stopped. The music was silenced. David was angry! What went wrong?

Anticipate a Time of Shaking

Let's look closely at a very important piece of information in this story. Nothing went wrong until they came to a place of *shaking*. The threshing floor was a place where the grain was shaken to remove the impure from the pure. For a season of time it appeared everything was right. Success was in sight. But suddenly, without warning, David's friend was dead.

It is foolish to wait until some moral or financial failure takes place to analyze the who, what, when, where and why of your life. Much like an automobile that is due for its checkup and oil change, it would be reckless to keep driving it until it begins to clamor with engine breakdown. Yet, so often we never stop to ask, "How should I go about this?" or "What are the proper steps for me to take?"

There may well be things in your life right now that are

not what God intends. Don't allow your temporary success to deceive you into believing that God has changed the pattern and is now allowing your end to justify the means. Search your heart and find the heart of God. Your destiny is at stake. Who wants to waste time and energy only to come to a place of shaking and find out that the pattern was wrong from the start?

The ark was to be carried on the shoulders of anointed priests, borne by poles placed through the rings that were attached to its side—never on an oxcart! (See Numbers 4:4–16.)

IT IS ONLY WHEN WE BECOME ANGRY AND SHUT OUR EARS TO LISTENING THAT WE LIMIT OUR ABILITY TO SUCCEED.

David's anger did not frustrate God or make his dream any less possible. It did bring him to a place of honest inquiry. Sometimes we have to come to the end of ourselves—get sick and tired of being sick and tired—before we really begin to pursue the wisdom of God and divine order.

Loved one, God can handle your frustration if He knows it comes from the heart of a seeker! It is only when we become angry and shut our ears to listening that we limit our ability to succeed. If some part of your life has been shaken and something died in the effort to steady it, don't quit. Investigate why. Be willing to ask the hard questions.

David asked, "How can the ark of the Lord come to

me?" One of the hallmarks of his life was the fact that he
was willing to inquire.

> One thing I have desired of the LORD,
> That will I seek...
> To behold the beauty of the LORD,
> And to inquire in His temple.
>
> —PSALM 27:4

Our strategies for victory will be birthed in our time
with the Lord. God has a plan for you. He will show you
how to succeed. All you have to do is inquire...ask!

> If any of you lacks wisdom, let him ask of God,
> who gives to all liberally and without reproach.
>
> —JAMES 1:5

God's plans and patterns come into view when we ask
Him. At the same time, we must realize that He uses
people to speak His principles into our lives. You must not
be afraid to interact with those He has placed in your life.
They cannot make your dreams come to pass for you, but
they can encourage you, correct you, admonish you and
instruct you in the ways of the Lord. They will help to
stimulate what God has put inside of you.

When we strive for clarity and understanding, God
reveals His order. We learn from our mistakes. Instead of
going in circles or dancing in a parade that is fruitless, we
realize our potential when God's order is revealed. After
Uzzah's death, David took three months to seek God's
order. But he found it! He learned that priests were to
carry the ark. *He made the adjustments!* He refused to allow
his bump in the road to become a roadblock to his dream.

What bumps are you facing? Has something in your life

that you thought was stable entered a time of shaking? Remember that there can be no celebration of victory until God's order has been established in your life.

Four Keys to Finding God's Order

As I have traveled throughout the nations of the world I have made the observation that a lack of significant progress or fruitfulness is often the indicator that something may be wrong. At the least, it is time to sit down and make an accurate assessment of what is going on. I want to offer four simple points to consider so that you can make the corrections necessary to succeed.

1. Remember

It is important that we go back to the original vision that God gave to us. Proverbs 29:18 declares, "Where there is no vision, the people perish" (KJV). The literal interpretation of *perish* is to "cast off restraint." If you attempt to live your life without God's vision for it, you lose your directive and wander in futility or empty pursuits.

For many Christians this does not necessarily indicate a lack of *motion*. It does indicate clearly a lack of *purpose*. Refresh your memory. What did God say to you in the beginning? What was the mandate that He gave to you?

2. Review

It is time to review your performance. Be honest with yourself as you look at what you have done, are doing or intend to do. After assessing his progress at fulfilling the mandate on his life, the apostle Paul wrote, "Brethren, I do not count myself to have apprehended…" (Phil. 3:13).

Proverbs 24:3–4 says:

> Any enterprise is built by wise planning, becomes
> strong through common sense, and profits won-
> derfully by keeping abreast of the facts.
>
> —TLB

3. Revise

When the plan you are using is not working, don't be
afraid to make changes. Acts 3:19 says, "Repent therefore
and return…" (NAS). This indicates that a change of
direction is needed. You cannot ignore the truth you have
discovered in your reviewing of the situation. You are
now confronted with a decision. Change, or march on
into disaster.

Often in my life I have thought I understood something
from the Lord only to realize later that I had misunderstood His directions or His timing. Many years ago, soon
after the Lord began to open doors for travel throughout
the world, I was so anxious to fulfill my destiny that I did
not wait for His divine order or timing.

We were scheduled to do a crusade in Jamaica. I was
excited about the meeting, especially in light of the fact
that our previous meeting there had been accompanied by
supernatural miracles. I arranged for a team of nearly fifty
people to travel with me for ten days of crusade meetings.
We had raised a substantial amount of money, spent time
training people in ministry, shouted the victory at the
send-off service and arrived ready to shake the island.
There was only one problem!

God had spoke to me sometime earlier that I was to
build relationships, not an itinerary. He also instructed me
to visit only those places to which He sent me. Invitations

alone were not enough to constitute a visit from our ministry team. In my excitement I did not take the time to pray these instructions through properly, nor to investigate the people with whom we were ministering.

GO ONLY WHERE GOD IS SENDING YOU.

When our ministry team arrived in Jamaica, I discovered that all the funds we had sent ahead of us to pay for the sponsoring of the crusade had been misused. Some local Christians had used the funds for other personal items. The crusade had never been advertised. The first night of the crusade there were more in attendance from our team than from the city where we were to preach. I was frustrated, angry and discouraged.

I went to prayer to complain to the Lord. "Why did You let this happen? These people have sacrificed to come, and saints have given their money for these meetings. How could You let this happen?"

Very quietly and quickly, God let me know that *He* did not do this—*I did*. He said to me, "I never sent you on this trip." With that one statement, all my arguments ended. I had failed to inquire of the Lord for His direction. Presuming that He would just bless whatever I did since I was doing it in His name was a grave mistake on my part.

As we reviewed the situation, I knew that I needed to revise our plans. The first thing I did was repent—to God and those with me. God forgave me and even turned what could have been a total disaster into something fruitful. But I learned a valuable lesson that has been a core value

of our ministry philosophy since then: Go only where
God is sending you.

4. Restructure

Saying you want to change and changing are two
entirely different things. In many cases the spirit is willing, but the flesh is weak. You may have to reorganize your
financial priorities, redefine your personal assignments,
prioritize your time more and find a new structure or system for governing. David had to find a new way to bring
the ark to Jerusalem. The old pattern was one of death and
destruction.

You may be locked up in old habits and patterns that
are destroying your ability to reach a place of significance
in life. There must be a willingness to reorder what isn't
working.

Could it be that the shaking you are experiencing is just
revealing those areas that need your attention? Don't
approach your bump as a mountain that cannot be overcome. Don't run and hide in fear that you have displeased
the Lord and now He will not help you. Get up and face
the facts. Change is needed! God will give you the ability
to cope with the changes that are needed. He will put you
on the road to dancing and rejoicing again. Don't stop par-
tying—find out the proper way to party!

chapter six

Becoming a Giant Killer

E very invitation into greatness is accompanied with obstacles and mountains that have to be faced. Adversity is nothing more than an incubator to process the destiny of men and women who are going to change the course of history. My friend Mike Murdock says that every believer will be known for the enemies they defeat or the enemies that defeat them.

Many times the very problems we think are going to destroy us become the platform for our promotion. We don't like to admit it, but we need an enemy in our life. The enemies we face make us aware of areas of need in our lives that we would never have recognized had we not faced the enemy. Some of the greatest discoveries made in

89

our lifetime came as the result of adversaries that sought our demise. Who knows if we would have heard of David had there not been a Goliath...or of Moses had there not been a Pharaoh.

Your friends create comfort, but your adversaries bring creative movement. It is not until we get tired of being harassed or taunted that we rise up with decisive action to begin the process of maturity and growth. Creativity... boundaries...strategies are all born when a "giant" appears in our pathway. Our willingness to respond releases God's power on our behalf.

More Than Survival

People in our world live in one of three spheres of life:

- Caught in cycles of survival
- Functioning in arenas of success
- Arriving at places of significance

Suffice it to say, believers are on a journey to significance. The abundant life of Jesus Christ allows you to hit the mark of purpose and destiny with joy in the journey!

Yet, many believers are living in survival. They are "saved, sanctified and filled with the Holy Ghost," but they are living from paycheck to paycheck, relationship to relationship, going from church to church—caught in a cycle of frustration and disappointment. Their lives have become one big fight! The abundant life of Jesus is something they see happening in others, but it seems foreign to their lives. Although they love God, giants continue to rob them of the vitality of life and the fruitfulness they desire.

There is good news for every stressed-out survivor. If

you are in a struggle, but you still have some "fight" inside, that is a sure sign you have not been defeated. Your spirit man knows you were not meant to live at that level of life and is pushing you toward your destiny.

YOUR FRIENDS CREATE COMFORT, BUT YOUR ADVERSARIES BRING CREATIVE MOVEMENT.

I know what it is to fight giants that have come to hinder my progress and try to force me into boundaries of limitation and isolation. Several years ago my wife, Kathy, and I experienced one of the most devastating attacks of the enemy against our lives and ministry. People we had trusted and loved had targeted us with their bitterness and refusal to progress. While experiencing breakthroughs and fresh anointing on one hand, we were being taunted and harassed on the other. Our adversary, who knew *infancy is the greatest season of vulnerability*, was challenging our destiny! Today, it is not shocking to me that even David, after having been anointed king, was brought to a place of confronting a *giant*. However, in those days I thought I was finished...washed up... "I'm outta here." I even prayed to die! Dying, it seemed to me, would have felt better than living.

My confrontation with giants took place shortly before we had taken our family to the mountains for our annual Christmas vacation. While there, I slipped back into the bedroom and got back into bed, not wanting to face my family or the future. While trying to reason with the Lord, the voice of the enemy was heckling my mind. All I could think about was the challenge of these giants.

I whispered a prayer to God, "Father, I am empty, and I don't know what to do. It seems that my enemies have triumphed over me. Maybe I only thought I was called to this place. Somehow, take away this pain inside me."

As tears began to roll down my checks, I heard the Spirit of God speak inside me. It was not with blowing trumpets or a cloud of smoke, but just a quiet voice, the kind that infuses your spirit with hope. The Lord said to me, "The anointing that is in you is stronger than any force trying to bind you. Get up...fresh oil is on the way." At that moment I recognized that I was born to conquer those giants. This mountain was going to prove to be the battlefield of victory for my future.

I got up, talked to my wife who had stood by me so faithfully, and we decided, "We cannot run from this Goliath. We must face it head-on."

It's pretty normal to desire to run from trouble in life. When you get up in the morning and the voice of your oppressor speaks loudly in your ear, taunting you, daring you to come out or make advancement, it is not unnatural to yearn to crawl back in bed and pull the covers over your head.

That is what happened to Saul and the soldiers who fought with him. Every morning they got up and *dressed for battle* and went out *shouting the war cry* (1 Sam. 17:20–21). When Goliath challenged them, they ran in fear to their tents and hid.

How often have you gone out, dressed for the part and saying the right things, only to retreat at the first sign of opposition? Saul's warriors ran to their tents, but we run to our places of self-protection and safety. Places of refuge where we will not be confronted or challenged. Comfort zones...where we make habitual choices, sound progressive, but end up going nowhere!

Comfort zones are no protection against giants. Neither is running *from* the giant. If you don't run *toward* the giant and overcome it, you will find yourself running into a life of make-believe success and significance. Before long you will find out that your success and significance are nothing more than tattered, worn-out "tents."

Never forget that life is full of options. Too many times we become so ritualized in our thinking that we accept whatever conditions are handed out as our portion in life. The old adage, "If the Lord wants me to have it, He'll give it to me," becomes the motto of the fearful and complacent. That makes about as much sense as saying, "If the Lord wanted my hair combed, He'd comb it."

COMFORT ZONES ARE NO PROTECTION AGAINST GIANTS.

Too often we end up spending years working for the same company, deceiving ourselves into believing it is loyal to us, only to find out that we are expendable and replaceable before tomorrow morning. We buy gas at the same place...eat at the same restaurants...hang on to dead relationships that are sucking the life out of us and failing to bring us one step closer to our destiny. We do this all because we are fearful of choosing something different. The giant has us on the run...hiding in fear!

Vince Lombardi once said, "Winning and losing...they are both habits!" Sometimes our lives degenerate into dysfunctional cycles because we refuse to deal with issues that arise, develop priorities or make decisions. Thus habits of running from issues are developed. We run from marriage, jobs, church and even our dreams. It is up to you to throw off the garbage that is keeping you from becoming the world changer God intends you to be.

The army of Saul that day reflected the attitude prevalent in much of our culture today—*rather than fighting the giant and risking failure, we just play the part.* The fear of failure is a major cause of our hesitancy and withdrawal from the battle—the lifestyle of a faithless non-risk taker.

WHEN WE LEARN THE PRINCIPLES NECESSARY TO DEVELOP OVERCOMING FAITH, THEN WE ARE NO LONGER HELD CAPTIVE BY EVERY PROBLEM THAT ARISES IN OUR LIFE.

As I write this I am in Honolulu, Hawaii for a national conference. Just a few miles from my hotel is Pearl Harbor, one of the greatest historic military sites in the world. As I reflected on the days in 1941 when foreign invaders suddenly attacked our nation, I understood the sudden burst of fear that swept this island and our entire nation. What was thought to be a safe place had suddenly been thrown into chaos and devastation. A giant had come forward to challenge our nation.

Our president at that time in history, Franklin D. Roosevelt, was a man acquainted with challenges and giants. Having overcome his own personal physical limitations to become elected, he assumed the office of the president at the height of the Great Depression. He knew that internal fortitude was needed to become an overcomer in the face of grave difficulties. In his inaugural address, he declared to America, "Let me assert my firm belief that the only thing we have to fear is fear itself...(the) terror which paralyzes needed efforts to convert retreat into advance."[1] It was his strong spirit that convinced our nation to fight on the land and on the sea. America had tried to avoid being involved in a "world war," but now she had to decide—run or stand up and face the giant!

Develop Your Strategy

If you are going to defeat the enemy that is taunting you, a successful strategy has to be developed. Many times we want God to defeat our giants, but God desires to empower us with creative strategies for victory. When we learn the principles necessary to develop overcoming faith, then we are no longer held captive by every problem that arises in our life. We *are* depending on Him to help us, but make no mistake—He wants us to get on the field!

We have to make the hard choices. We are the ones who have to pursue wisdom. God's promise is to "make the way of escape" (1 Cor. 10:13). Our job is to find it. When we keep that goal in mind, we will be willing to work through the temporary discomfort of feeling insecure or inadequate and get to work. Here are some simple guidelines for developing the heart of a giant killer.

Ask the proper questions.
Conjecture and assumption are not the proper grounds

for battle. Too many people are *fighting battles that have no spoils*. In order to steward our time and avoid making a bad investment, we must learn to assess the situation by asking the proper questions. If not, we will find ourselves distracted by pettiness, and we will lose ground in our journey.

Knowing how to ask the right questions is a secret to drawing out the facts that are needed to become successful in your conquest. How many times have you been embarrassed to ask a question for fear that you were being simple or asking dumb questions? We are afraid that others will laugh at our ignorance. Or we retreat from asking because we are afraid those listening will misinterpret our intentions and judge us wrongfully. However, there are no dumb questions. Information is necessary to make the decisions necessary to move toward our victory.

> For which of you, intending to build a tower, does not sit down first and count the cost, whether he has enough to finish it?
>
> —LUKE 14:28

David asked the question, "What will be done for the man who kills this giant?" He wanted to know if there were spoils of victory that would come to him for his efforts.

Have you ever met people who seem to live for conflict? They are constantly fighting over stuff that does not even mean anything. They are always drawing their sense of identity from having to win at something constantly. Their combative nature, when combined with their competitive spirit, traps them in cycles of continual crisis. Most of the time these people are never taken seriously and are avoided by people. Because they never learn to choose their battles wisely, they waste time, energy and resources with no obvious return. It becomes a bad investment of their lives.

David was not going to fight just to be in a fight. He wanted spoils. He was going to evaluate the investment and be sure that it was worth his effort. And he received an answer to his question.

> The king will give great wealth to the man who kills him. He will also give him his daughter in marriage and will exempt his father's family from taxes in Israel.
>
> —1 SAMUEL 17:25, NIV

When David realized that the reward for killing the Philistine included riches, marrying into the king's family and never having to pay taxes again, it was easy to make his decision.

Are you in conflict over things in your life, but know that when the battle is over there will be nothing to show for it? Whatever this conflict is, it is robbing you of your effectiveness.

Refuse to allow others to control your destiny.

Take confident charge of your life. Refuse to be intimidated by the opinions or criticisms of others. At times the people who are closest to you feel qualified to know what is best for you without ever considering your God-ordained purpose. They view you through eyes of preconceived judgments that are based on what they *knew you to be* rather than on *who God is making you to be now.*

There are, it may be, so many kinds of voices in the

world, and none of them is without signification.

—1 CORINTHIANS 14:10, KJV

You must realize that there are many voices in your world. All of them vie for your attention and seek to shape your life. Some call you higher; others are leading you into paths of self-destruction, seeking their own agendas. Learn to discern them, and refuse to be controlled by wrong voices. Every day you must sort through all of the sounds, both internal and external, that scream for your attention— your schedules and responsibilities, your dreams and visions, your families and your failures. Each of these things will try to determine your future.

There were many voices in David's life that day. His boss was telling him he was too young. His adversary was calling him names and cursing him by his Philistine gods. His brothers were critical of his motives. And the soldiers were questioning his intelligence to want to fight this giant. Each voice was a sound of criticism.

Not everyone is going to be thrilled with your choice to fight and win. The loudest and most obnoxious voice of all comes from the critics, those "Monday morning quarterbacks" who spend their lives sitting in the safety of the grandstands and never taking a risk or developing the discipline to get into the game on the field. They are trivial in their attitude toward life, missing the beauty of the journey because of the bugs on the window!

Don't misunderstand me here; we all need people who will speak into our lives, challenge our decisions and impart wisdom to us. I am not talking about the people who watch over your life and seek your good. I'm referring to people who continually find something wrong with everything you do—those faultfinders who always seem to know what you are doing wrong and why you won't succeed. They are not people with whom you are unfamiliar; often they are those who are closest to you. Many times they come from within our own households. When you have people in your life who know where you came from and still believe in you and your dream, these people are gifts from God to you!

David's brothers shot barbs at him. They questioned his motives and asked why he was not tending to his menial job of shepherding. Why had he come down to the battlefield that day? Who did he think he was? Had he forgotten where he came from?

There is no way to know the real source of their contention, but it appears to be born of jealousy more than anything else. When the prophet Samuel had come to their father's house to anoint another king, each of them had been called in for the meeting. While many of them looked the part, Samuel was not moved to anoint any of them as king. Samuel was not rejecting their worth or giftings, but God had not chosen any of them as the future king. He had chosen the least likely candidate—David.

It is not unusual for those who have felt rejection to become seedbeds of anger and hostility toward anyone doing the things they had hoped to do. Instead of rising to discover their abilities and find their place, they find it much easier to run with the crowd and take verbal stabs at those who are doing the stuff! Their anger robs them of their ability to celebrate others and keeps their lives void of joy.

David's brothers were obnoxious, verbal and open with their disdain. His willingness to fight against such incredible odds shined a spotlight on what they perceived to be their own flaws and shortcomings. It is likely that their jealousy and resentment were rooted in their own awareness of their unfulfilled dreams.

His leader, on the other hand, was a bit more sophisticated in his smugness. King Saul, who had begun to experience his own sense of rejection due to his unwillingness to heed God's command, was not openly sarcastic. But he was suspicious of David's ability. He told David he was too young and too inexperienced to fight the giant.

Goliath was another story altogether. He mocked David. He viewed him as an unworthy opponent who would be destroyed in moments. It was insulting to him that they would send a boy to fight a man's battle.

Learning to deal with all these voices and not allowing them to determine the course of your life is a key to completing your journey to significance. Most people are far more in love with the image of success than with the process of becoming successful.

Most dreams do not die in the visionary stage. We all want fulfillment and fruitfulness. I don't know of a single person who is not at least interested in talking about how to make his or her life impacting. The vision is exhilarating! It is implementation of the vision that becomes difficult. When our prophetic promise has to be lived out in a world filled with pressure, problems and voices that question our existence and mock our abilities, that is when we hesitate to move forward.

I am grateful that God allowed me to go through the painful days of stress and rejection from those who were closest to me when I was in the early years of ministry. The internal development that came as a result of it helped me to develop immunity to the "everybody-is-talk-ing-about-me" syndrome. If it had not been for His grace working in me, toughening me up, I would have run away in fear.

It is important to recognize that David did not deal with each of these voices in the same manner. His ability to discern their intent and to respond was an important step in his journey. It became a matter of survival and success.

When David's brothers began to question him and bring attacks against him publicly, David had to make a choice. At that point he could have allowed his emotions to drive his behavior. While we can never totally remove our emotions from the decisions we make, we must never allow them to become the compass by which we operate. So in response to Eliab, David chose to ignore his comments and walk away. Instead, he reminded Eliab that there was a cause that day in Israel. The safety and future of the nation were at stake. He was not living just for himself, but asking questions to determine what could be done.

> To sum up...not returning evil for evil, or insult for insult, but giving a blessing instead; for you were called for the very purpose that you might inherit a blessing. For, "Let him who means to love life and see good days refrain his tongue from evil and his lips from speaking guile."
>
> —1 PETER 3:8–10, NAS

When those around you don't believe you can do it... walk on! Stop trying to convince people who will never be persuaded that you are called, anointed or talented. You are wasting time and energy. Get up and get going! In spite of your prayers for God to reveal your heart to them, they still don't believe you. They may never change—but you are going to change. You are going to break free from dependency on their approval and move into new realms of growth and success.

Someone may ask, "What about the *Sauls* in my life? What do I do when those who are in authority over me refuse to 'give me my shot'?"

At this point in the relationship between David and Saul, there was no personal animosity. There was just a limited amount of information for Saul concerning David's credentials. And, although Saul was the king, he too had been overtaken in fear, withdrawing from the fight. As he faced this young Hebrew boy who was willing to confront the giant, David became a reminder to Saul of what he had refused to be!

WHEN THOSE AROUND YOU DON'T BELIEVE YOU CAN DO IT...WALK ON!

When Saul questioned his experience and age, David did not respond in rebellion or arrogance. He took the time to relate to Saul his recent foray into fighting *giants*. He told of his responsibility to care for his father's sheep. He described to Saul how he had defeated the lion and the bear.

It is important for every young man or woman who desires to move forward in God's plan to allow time for those who are over you in the Lord to view your track record and bring you to a place of promotion. David was not being self-promoting; he was merely sharing what

God had done in his life on the backside of the hills of Judea. His patient explanation opened the door to his opportunity. There will be those who have judged you based only on what they assume to be true about you by observation and whose hearts will be changed when they understand your days of processing!

Be who God made you to be.

Once Saul understood that David's willingness to fight was born out of proven faithfulness, not just blind faith, he tried to fit him with his clothes. Far too often people who mentor you will try and force you into a mold of being just like them, a clone, rather than simply developing the gifts within you while allowing for your uniqueness and personal identity.

The temptation is to wear someone else's clothes or to attempt to fulfill the will of God for your life with someone else's anointing or abilities. Be who God called you to be. Recognize the things that you do well, and do them. If God made you an original, why spend your entire life trying to be a copy? Take the things that you have proven and use them to change your destiny.

Run to the roar.

Don't cower in timidity from the mocking voices of your Goliaths—run at them instead. It was customary in David's day for the two opposing champion warriors to confront each other verbally before the battle began. They would challenge their opponent in the name of the gods they served or belittle one another in an effort to drain each other of confidence.

While watching a nature show on television one day, I discovered that the same pattern prevails in the animal kingdom among lions. They use a pattern of intimidation to frighten the prey they are hunting into a trap they have set up. Then they are able to overtake that prey. The pattern is for an old lion that is no longer able to run fast or conquer large game to stand on one side of the field while all the younger lionesses line up on the other side. Because of his age, the old lion has a much more ferocious roar, and when a little gazelle comes near, the old lion begins to roar. In fear the gazelle will begin to *run away*, heading in the opposite direction away from the roar. What it does not realize is that it is running directly into the trap that has been set. The young lionesses pounce on it and destroy it.

That is what happens in the life of many Christians. The devil continually harasses them, draining them of confidence until they run away from their moment of breakthrough and into a trap the enemy has set for them to bind them from their place of significance. Don't be fooled...run to the roar. Run with understanding.

IF GOD MADE YOU AN ORIGINAL, WHY SPEND YOUR ENTIRE LIFE TRYING TO BE A COPY?

The thing that made Goliath so intimidating was the fact that his reputation preceded his actual appearance. He was huge in physical stature. He had been a warrior since his youth and had never lost a battle. The mention of *his name* struck fear in the hearts of the mightiest of men.

We have enemies in our lives that taunt us with their proven reputations—those things in life that people seem never to recover from. When people hear the words *divorce...abuse...bankruptcy...rape...job cutbacks...cancer*...they are overcome with fear. The enemy knows how these things intimidate us, and he shouts all the louder.

If we keep our mouths shut during those hours of intimidation we will be defeated. It is not a time for *explanation*, but rather a *declaration*. Like David, we have to realize that we also have something to say. Our God has a mighty reputation! He has never lost a battle...never suffered a setback...and is all powerful!

> Who is like Thee among the gods, O LORD?
> Who is like Thee, majestic in holiness,
> Awesome in praises, working wonders?
>
> —EXODUS 15:11, NAS

Never run at your giants *with your mouth shut!* That is a formula for defeat. Declare *His name*...Jesus! The mention of His name causes the forces of hell to tremble!

With his simple slingshot and a mouth full of confidence, David ran toward Goliath. With one release of the stone, the giant fell. David ran and cut his head off for the king. A great victory had been won!

Friends, if you are always weeping over criticism and rejection, continually frustrated because somebody misunderstood you, or upset because some group of friends won't let you in their group anymore, you must make the choice to break free today! Your progress and future potential demand it. Don't allow the voices of a few to rob you of His voice saying, "Well done!"

chapter seven

Learning to Behave in a Cave

F aithfulness always brings increased opportunities! For those who are diligent, doors will open that remain closed for those who approach their purpose in life haphazardly. However, faithfulness does not always generate the promised promotion we desire in the manner or time frame we always expect it. Sometimes the way up is down.

Along with the increased opportunities there are increased struggles and disappointments. There are times that no matter what we do, it seems that everything is going wrong. We pray...we fast...yet, adversity still seems to come to our lives.

Someone has said, "Success breeds success," and I certainly agree that the momentum of fruitfulness is a valuable

107

asset in everyone's life. But we must also admit that success creates a whole new set of issues in a person's life. Before you were promoted, everyone enjoyed your company, laughed at your jokes and told you their troubles. Now that you, like the television sitcom character George Jefferson, have "moved on up to the East Side," your advancement has become a magnet for obstacles and difficult people. Friends with whom you once had close fellowship now withdraw from you due to their own insecurities and hidden jealousy. People who once helped you up stand off in the corner and talk about you, criticizing your newly experienced success. Your promotion will demand that you go to a new level of maturity.

NEITHER THE CIRCUMSTANCES OF LIFE NOR THE STRATEGIES OF HELL CAN ABORT GOD'S PURPOSES.

Temporary setbacks become your opportunities for evaluating your progress and for making a fresh commitment to God's purpose for you. General Douglas MacArthur once said, "War does not make a man a hero or a coward. It just proves which one he is." God's kingdom operates according to times and seasons. Not every day is "party day," and not every day is a trial—there are seasons of both. Your greatest struggle will be waiting for your *season* of destiny to manifest.

Martin Luther King Jr. once made the statement: "The greatness of a man cannot be seen in the hours of comfort and convenience, but rather in the moments of conflict and adversity." You must never forget that destiny is fashioned during the process of learning to walk in faith and humility during each season of your life. If you are enjoying tremendous accomplishments, walk humbly before God as you realize it is His work in you that is making it possible. If delays and detours have appeared on your journey, remain confident that what He has spoken, He is able and willing to perform.

> ...being fully assured that what He had promised,
> He was able also to perform.
>
> —ROMANS 4:21, NAS

> I am watching over My word to perform it.
>
> —JEREMIAH 1:12, NAS

> And we know that God causes all things to work together for good to those who love God, to those who are called according to His purpose.
>
> —ROMANS 8:28, NAS

When we are in one of those detours that are meant for our development but seems to be destroying our focus, we must remember that God is working according to purpose. Neither the circumstances of life nor the strategies of hell can abort God's purposes. For David, it meant *learning to behave in a cave!*

After David's successful defeat of Goliath and sudden rise to fame, it became obvious that not everyone was pleased. The nation celebrated him while those close to him sought his demise. He was living in what Charles Dickens once described as "the best of times and the worst of times." I used to wonder, *How can life be good and bad at the same time?* But as I have walked through my own personal journey to fulfill the purposes of God for my life, it has become evident that dichotomy is a reality.

When Trouble Follows Victory

I am sure David was delighted with the anointing that had touched his life and transformed him, taking him from a shepherd boy to national prominence. At the same time he was probably confused over why his victory created such trouble with those around him. Had he not helped the nation defeat one of its greatest enemies? Had he not brought the head of Goliath back for Saul? Why all the trouble?

David's story is no different from the story of many people in our time who face similar experiences in the corporate business world in which they live and function. Many are working hard for the companies that employ them, giving of themselves tirelessly, only to find out that their efforts have created envy and backbiting among the very people they are helping to make successful. What happens when your supervisor becomes threatened by your sudden favor? Could it be that your diligence and promotion are irritating simply because they are reminding your supervisor of things he or she was unwilling to do or become in order to fulfill his or her own dreams?

Martin Luther King Jr. was a strategic change agent in our nation. Most of what he dreamed about didn't happen until after his untimely death from an assassin's bullet. It is important to understand why he was viewed as a threat. Sure, times were different. Yes, tensions were running high. But the reality is that Dr. King, the son of a Baptist preacher, born in the South during the height of racial bigotry when membership in the white supremacist group the KKK had its highest membership, was not a threat because he promoted violence or was a communist agent. He was a threat because he took a stand against racism and segregation and forced the American people to face their own declared values of "liberty and justice for all."

When David's popularity began to increase, Saul did not understand the source of David's success. He only knew *he* was losing popularity. His own character flaws were becoming evident when compared to David's determined faith and continued success.

> So David went out wherever Saul sent him, and behaved wisely. And Saul set him over the men of war, and he was accepted in the sight of all the people and also in the sight of Saul's servants... And David behaved wisely in all his ways, and the LORD was with him. Therefore, when Saul saw that he behaved very wisely, he was afraid of him.
>
> —1 SAMUEL 18:5, 14–15

What about those faithful church members who work hard in the church they attend—serving on committees, working with the children, doing the outreaches—only to discover that they have become the topic of conversation throughout the congregation. Their intentions have been misinterpreted and maligned. As a result, their hearts become full of confusion over the course their life has taken. Often the actions of envious people create divided loyalties, strained relationships and betrayal. People are forced to choose between those who are experiencing the favor of the Lord and those who are fighting to save their position.

When David found himself being sought by Saul and his army to be killed, he realized he had become a marked man. He fled to the cave of Adullam.

You may think at first that his actions could be perceived as cowardly. But how do you respond when your success is creating bitter jealousy and murderous actions from those you are trying to serve? What do you do the morning after you discover that you were released from your assignment because others had plotted against you and misrepresented your actions?

You would probably do what David did. You run to a place of refuge—a cave! It was there in that lonely cave that the next stage on David's journey to significance would take place. In is in your cave experience that you will take your own next step toward significance.

God's Holding Pattern

The caves of Adullam are large openings in the mountains of Judea where men who were running for their lives or away from creditors would hide out. These caves, which for many were nothing more than a hiding place, became for David a secret place of intimacy and revelation.

We all enjoy the seasons of exposure when God takes us to the front of the class and demonstrates His awesome power through us. It is wonderful to slay a giant in front of all your fellow countrymen—including those brothers who mocked you as they sat down in cowardice. However, the real test comes when God hides you, when your dreams and visions, along with your promotion, are put in a holding pattern.

Recently I was flying back to Florida on a Delta airline

flight. Our takeoff had been delayed for two hours due to a bad thunderstorm that had shut down the airport. We had begun boarding before the storm arrived and were not allowed to deplane. We had to sit it out from our seats in the plane, which was sitting on the runway.

No matter what class of service you fly in, sitting in an airplane seat for two hours in a plane that is sitting on a runway is a real test of patience. Finally, we took off. Once we were airborne, I was eager to arrive at our destination. After all, the delay had already taken more time than the flight itself was scheduled to do. However, once we began our approach into Atlanta, where I needed to make a connecting flight, the pilot came over the audio system to announce that air traffic control in Atlanta had instructed him to go into a "holding pattern." We would have to wait to land. Wait? In the air? You must be kidding. That is a strange place to start waiting!

People became restless and even a bit nervous. However, everyone's fears were set aside when the pilot came back on the intercom system to remind those traveling that the reason we had returned to the departure terminal before we left was to refuel before embarking on our flight. He reassured everyone that the airlines always prepared for such situations and that the plane carried enough fuel. He was giving valuable information for those who were serious about making the journey.

Cave time is often waiting time! The struggle of our faith comes in not knowing how long we must wait. It is during the times when God puts us in a holding pattern, showing us only an uncertain future, that our walk demands we step forward on two legs—the legs of faith and patience.

> That you may not be sluggish, but imitators of
> those who through faith and patience inherit the
> promises.
>
> —HEBREWS 6:12, NAS

It takes faith and patience to make this journey. When God's delays take place in your life, don't become passive or complacent. The word *sluggish* implies lost momentum and lost passion. If you are in a holding pattern, you must determine in your heart that you will not become stagnant or indifferent.

Before the delay, you may have felt that you were on the verge of something spectacular. You are! God has not changed His mind about you. He is at work *preparing you for what He has prepared for you!*

While in the cave you become skilled at being faithful even though you may be experiencing personal need. The most difficult time of faith is during the waiting period when it seems nothing is working. It becomes easy to use your personal difficulties as an excuse for why you are not fulfilling the destiny of your life. Instead of making your world different as a result of your faithfulness in adversity, you may be tempted to say, "I'm struggling right now," or "It seems like nothing is working for me at the present, so I am just going to step back for a while." No! Understand what is happening and learn how to conduct yourself in those conditions. As Richard Phillips said in his book *The Heart of an Executive*, "...the man who would be king must act the part even when he is not wearing the crown."[1]

It is amazing that during some of the most distressful days of your life, God will send people to you who are worse off than you are. You may want to feel sorry for yourself and have a pity party, but people show up at your door wanting your help. You must recognize that *the anointing will always attract needs.*

When you are anointed with favor, people are drawn to you. David was becoming a national hero, a man of destiny. People who were desperate for a change were observing his promotion and being drawn to him.

Isn't it frustrating that when you want to run and hide and lick your wounds, God sends people to you who need what you have? You feel empty and confused, yet they come to you for help. David probably thought, *I can't help you... I need help!* But that was what the holding pattern he was in was all about. God was working according to His purposes. David was going to need an army of mighty men, and here they were. They did not look like an army, but they were the soil into which David would sow his own life, and they would become radically transformed as a result.

Cave Etiquette 101

As difficult as the process may be, there are several keys to learning how to behave in a cave. Let's take a look at the elements of our spiritual code of behavior for cave experiences.

Decide to survive.

When you find yourself in your cave, decide right then and there that *you will survive!* Determine from the start that the waiting and the disappointment will not destroy you. You may be struggling to understand and find your direction, but it is important to tell yourself continually that *this too will pass.* Don't allow the pressure of the present to force you into developing a pessimistic attitude or fatalism. *Never make permanent decisions based on temporary circumstances.*

It is obvious from David's activities that he would do whatever it took to survive. He had feigned insanity, made covenant with his enemy's son Jonathan and ran for his life—but in it all, he refused to quit. Because of his determined faith he did not fail to fulfill his destiny.

NEVER MAKE PERMANENT DECISIONS BASED ON TEMPORARY CIRCUMSTANCES.

You are not a failure simply because you fell down or suffered a setback. You may be in a recovery mode, or you may even be waiting for God's vindication. Refuse to be impulsive or reactive. In the process, it is important that you distinguish between the event—your failure—and your position in life. The development of the call of God that brought you to this place has not been lifted off your life.

> The steps of a good man are ordered by the LORD,
> And He delights in his way.
>
> —PSALM 37:23

> For the gifts and the calling of God are irrevocable.
>
> —ROMANS 11:29

David may have found himself in the cave of Adullam, but it is important to realize that he was no less of an anointed king there than he was the day Samuel poured the oil over his head. He was still God's anointed king!

Circumstances will arise in your life for which you are not prepared, but God's eye is still on you. You must purpose in your heart that, "Wherever I am, I am who God says I am. My identity is not based on my feelings or present circumstances, but on who He has declared me to be in Christ."

Evaluate your opportunities.

Another key principle to learning to behave in a cave is *learning to properly evaluate your opportunities.* The men who came to David while he was in the cave were discouraged, discontented, distressed and in debt. They were not on the all-star list of champions from Judea. Though these men did not appear to be prime candidates for army recruitment, they were future kingdom builders. Dysfunctional...lacking leadership and without focus... yet, men that God could use to shape a nation and establish His reign. *A diamond is still a diamond even if it is covered over with mud!*

If we are not careful, our times of testing and stretching can blind us to the possibilities that are around us and to the potential of those who are coming to our side. I have watched men and women chosen by God to lead people to new levels of thinking and fruitfulness became oblivious to the treasures around them due to the personal struggles they were facing. If you want to reach the place of significance that God has chosen for you, you must guard your heart from becoming self-absorbed. Preoccupation with injustices that are being leveled against you, or with the incompetence of those around you, will only soothe your fleshly emotions temporarily. And, more importantly, it will weaken your faith to stand. When you allow circumstances to blind you from the vision God has for you, distraction and forfeited destinies await you.

Often in an effort to hurry through a cave experience, we become overly eager to escape, focusing all of our attention on our own situation. But by doing that we become disconnected from the real purpose God has for processing us through the cave. We must remain faithful to our calling, even when the needs of our own lives are pressing in upon us.

Some believers feel slighted when adversity or detours interrupt their plans. For some reason they feel they have an "adversity exclusion clause" in their covenant. Their preoccupation with self has become a thief of the greatness that lies within them. Without proper discernment, they will miss the window of opportunity to strengthen their character. They will not be able to develop a vision for the potential of the mighty men who are gathering around them.

Express your worship.

In the period of time leading up to David's encampment in the cave at Adullam, he had written Psalm 34. It becomes a remedy for cave time, and it is the third key to proper cave decorum—*expressive worship*!

David begins his psalm by saying:

> I will bless the LORD at all times,
> His praise shall continually be in my mouth.
>
> —PSALM 34:1

When we replace our grumbling and complaining with praise, our cave will be transformed from a place of disappointment to a place of development. During the hours of loneliness and frustration, guard your words! Fill your mouth with praise. David said, "I will bless the Lord."

A heart of praise is an act of the human will. When God created man, He made him in the image of God, with God-like qualities. One of the attributes of mankind that is distinct from all other creative order is that man has volition. We have the ability to make choices...to will. The life of praise, which will change our environment and affect the atmosphere of our lives, is the result of our will being harnessed and focused.

When you face your cave experience, you choose the response you make. You can choose to be mad, to seek revenge for the rejection that has been inflicted upon you. Or you can choose to gossip and to tell secrets about those who have done you wrong. But if you are going to respond the way God wants you to respond, you will "will" to bless the Lord. Rather than using your lips to destroy yourself and others, choose to use your lips to honor the Lord!

There will come a point in your journey when you must declare, "I have too much will to die in this trouble. I have too much will to continue to be overtaken by depression." Declare your praise, and watch as the enemy begins to retreat from your thankful heart. *Willful praise is an indicator that faith is alive!*

Boast in the Lord.

In his psalm from out of the midst of his cave experience, David asserted:

> My soul shall make its boast in the LORD;
> The humble shall hear of it and be glad.
>
> —PSALM 34:2

David learned that our boasting is to be *in the Lord*. One

thing the cave does is to help strip us of our arrogance and self-sufficiency. We come to the place of recognizing that no matter how talented we may be, how many people are singing our songs, what the media is saying about us— "Saul has killed his thousands, David has killed his ten thousands"—without Jesus we would not make it. Whatever levels of effectiveness we reach, we have only arrived at the level so that we can lavish praise and honor on His name. Our pursuit of His presence is the beginning of a heart of worship!

If you are experiencing a time in your life when you need to overcome the loneliness of dreams that are not yet coming to pass, and those around you are acting as if you are unqualified to fulfill them, then recognize the pattern here—*boast in the Lord*. Don't try to convince people how wise you are. Don't boast in your giftedness or how you could help the situation. Stop trying to convince those who are unbelieving that you are an anointed king. Just brag on Him! Take time to make Him big in your day.

Granted, your praise may become irritating to some people. To those self-made people who think they pulled themselves up by their own bootstraps, someone who continually acknowledges the goodness of the Lord is like a stone in the heel of your shoe—they just don't wear good. Yet, those who are humble enough to recognize that Someone bigger is directing their paths are filled with joy when they hear your praise going up.

I heard the testimony of a single mother in Texas who was raising two sons. She did not have work at the time, yet she was responsible for providing for her children's needs. For many years, she had started her day in prayer. Her prayer life was not short, and it was not quiet. When she prayed, the neighbors knew she was praying.

After a few weeks, money got tight, and she had nothing with which to buy groceries. She did not tell her two sons. Instead, she fed them breakfast and sent them on to school. Once they left she began to pray. It was summer, and the weather was hot. Not wanting to run her air conditioning, she opened the windows in her house.

As she began to pray that day, she petitioned the Lord for food for her household. At the same time she was praying, the man who lived next door, who had always mocked this lady and her walk with God, heard her praying for provisions. He thought, *I'm going to show that old lady that God doesn't hear her prayers. I'm going to trick her.* He had been a practicing agnostic most of his life.

So he decided to go to the local grocery store and buy some groceries. Once he finished shopping, he went to the lady's house. Realizing that she would not see him, he slipped up on her porch and left four bags of groceries in front of the door. He knocked on the door and then ran around to the side of the house, waiting on her to come to the door.

When she opened the door, this desperate mother began shouting at the sight of those bags of groceries. She declared, "Thank You, Jesus! Thank You for providing for me. Thank You, Lord!"

About that time the neighbor came from the side of the house and said, "Hey, lady, what are you shouting about?"

She replied, "Sir, the Lord has answered my prayers. We had no food left in this house, and now God has provided for us."

"God didn't buy those groceries," he retorted back to her in an effort to mock her and discourage her. "I did!"

When she heard that, instead of feeling discouraged, she began to shout all the louder, "Glory to God... Hallelujah!" She even began to dance!

Frustrated, the man replied, "Now what are you shouting about?"

"Sir," she replied, "I am rejoicing because the Lord provided for my needs, and *he made the devil pay for it!*"

Friends, when we purpose in our hearts to boast in our God and His goodness, He will provide our needs and make the devil pay the bill!

Praise Transforms Your Cave—and You

Oh, magnify the LORD with me,
And let us exalt His name together.
—PSALM 34:3

In the midst of it all, David's heart cry was for God to get big! The principle of magnification is very simple. When you put a magnifying glass over top or in front of an object, your perception of the object is enlarged. You don't actually change the size of the object being observed; you just change your perspective of it. When you determine to behave in a cave with an attitude of gratitude and to lift up praise, you are magnifying the Lord. Just as the magnifying glass in front of an object doesn't change the size of the object, you don't change the size of God or His ability, but rather your perception of who He is and what He is doing in your life and circumstances changes.

Praise then becomes transforming! The greatest demonstration of the spirit of faith is when we release a song in the midnight hours of our life. Faith is seen in the heart of an individual who, while still in a cave, can begin to sing and declare, "God is good...all the time!" When hands that have become calloused by the struggles of life, both natural and spiritual, are lifted in praise, expressing the joy of a soul set free, God hears and "delivers us from all our fears." (See Psalm 34:4.) When fear is gone, the holding pattern will no longer crush our spirit.

The results were that David came out of the cave of Adullam with four hundred mighty men. They became one of the most efficient "Special Forces" in the military history of mankind. They defeated giants, took cities, broke through strongholds and established David's kingdom reign. They went from being financially broke to being well supplied, from being distressed to being focused.

That is why you cannot give up. You may have come to a place where circumstances have dealt you a setback. Maybe you feel as if your dreams are on hold. Talk to yourself. Open your mouth, and begin to change the atmosphere with your praise. The intensity of your worship will be born out of the ever-present awareness of that from which God has brought you and where He intends to take you. When that happens, you, like David, will say:

> Oh, taste and see that the LORD is good.
>
> —PSALM 34:8

The bitterness of the struggle will be replaced by the sweetness of His grace and the glory of His plan! You are on your way, learning to behave in a cave!

chapter eight

Built
for
Connection

I n our effort to succeed and to reach our goals in life, we often forget that one of the most important ingredients for a fruitful life is relationship. The anointing flows out of relationship. Whether it is our *vertical relationship* with the Lord or our *horizontal relationships* with other people, the opportunities opened to us and our ability to respond effectively are affected by our relationships.

While religion tries to turn our experience with Jesus into something rigid and legalistic, it is important to note that the call from Jesus to His first disciples was a call to relationship. The Word declares, "He appointed twelve, that they might be *with Him...*" (Mark 3:14, emphasis added). His first desire was fellowship and relationship, from which ministry would flow.

Today, Christ still desires a personal relationship with His people. Yet so many believers have lost the importance of a personal relationship with God in the midst of the pressures of life and because of the convenience of visiting someone else's revival. Recently Pastor Jack Hayford told a group of pastors, "If you ever lose your personal devotional life, you will eventually lose your ministry." Why? Because true ministry flows out of *being*, not *doing*.

Relationships demand that you deal with *who you are*— not necessarily with *what you do*. Often your "real self" is not the person you are projecting while standing on a platform in a ministry opportunity. Your real self is who you are behind closed doors in personal devotions and covenant relationships.

One day while ministering in Fiji, the late Ed Cole, former president of The Men's Network, said something to me that has impacted my life since that day. "Tony, the greatest assets you have in life are your friends. You can always get your money back…your house back…or even another job. But you can't always get your friends back." That day I realized that my ability to fulfill the mandate of God on my life would be greatly affected by my relationships.

TRUE MINISTRY FLOWS OUT OF BEING, NOT DOING.

In many places today, people are suffering. Not because they don't have a job or provisions…not because of abuse or neglect…but due to the reality of not having any friends. There is no one to go to lunch with, nobody to share their victories with and no one to cry with, so they have ended up living in a world of loneliness. They are cut off from the fellowship that cultivates nurturing and the cross-pollination that would bring the productivity for which they are longing.

God has appointed someone to your life. Whether it be one individual or several during the course of a lifetime, the people assigned for your success and promotion will be instrumental in bridging the gap between your dreams and their fulfillment. These individuals hold the keys that will unlock the dreams that are inside of you. They don't have to be famous, just appointed. Big doors swing on little hinges. It takes only the right connections for big things to happen in your life. For example, Ananias became the prophetic voice that connected Saul, who became Paul, to his miraculous deliverance from blindness and his insight to his destiny in ministry (Acts 9:1–19).

The wonderful thing about our relationships in the body of Christ is that our "connections" don't have to be developed at the expense of our integrity or morality. God guides people, who for the sheer joy of helping, come to our aid and counsel.

For far too long we have been content to "go it alone." Believing that somehow we could accomplish the purposes of God by ourselves, we have totally missed the fact that we are *one body...one church!* So we stay isolated by our dogmas and denominational creeds, separated by our styles and preferences and afraid of anyone that is not just like us. It has resulted in the church having a marginal impact on our cities and world at best.

Often I have heard Christians say, "Just me and Jesus... that's all it takes." The only problem is that God's plan for mankind and His purposes in the earth were never designed to be fulfilled by solo individuals. We were built for connection.

In Genesis 2:18, God looked down at Adam and declared, "It is not good that man should be alone." According to the biblical background of this period of history, we know that Adam was not alone. Each day God would come and walk in the Garden with him, fellowshiping and instructing him. Yet, God Himself determined that Adam, by himself, could never reach his fullest potential nor fulfill the eternal purposes of God. It was going to take relationship for stewardship to be completed.

So God said, "I will make a companion who will help him" (v. 18, NLT). And God fashioned Eve. She came from Adam, but yet she was not like him. She was unique... special... God's chosen partner for His first man. She had differing abilities and talents. She was not like him in her beauty or her physiology. She was constructed so that they could partner and be fruitful.

So often in our journey in life we try to establish relationships with people who are just like us—they think like us, talk like us, dress like us. However, we soon realize we are missing something—fruit! Just as Adam could not be fruitful by himself, or even with another person who was just like him, you and I can never reach our fullest potential without the proper relationships being built in our lives.

Many denominations and groups have become sterile in their growth and effectiveness because they refuse to "cross-pollinate." They listen only to people who are just like them. Continually drawing from the same spiritual gene pool, they end up with doctrines and practices that are handicapped and limited. If we do not change in our approach to building relationships across the body of Christ, we are going to limit our ability to impact this generation and shape the world.

On his journey to rulership in Zion, David came to a place called *Hebron* (1 Chron. 11:1–3). Hebron was a difficult to place to reach geographically. It was positioned in the rocky terrain of Israel. *Hebron* means "the seat of association or the place of joining." It represented a place of covenanting.

It is vital that we as believers learn the value of covenant and its effect in fulfilling the purposes of God in the earth. The men that came to David in Hebron were not weak, ineffective, unemployed men. They were strong, gifted men, leaders in their own right. Yet these men knew that they must lay down their personal agendas in order for Israel to become the nation God intended it to be. If they were to be able to defeat the enemies that sought to destroy them, they would have to covenant together with the man that God had chosen to lead the nation—David. Their partnership would produce the greatest time of victory and peace that Israel ever had. It enabled David to take back the throne in Jerusalem and to bring the ark of the covenant back to Zion.

Partnership is a strong word. It denotes a relationship that is greater than casual friendship or a "we-go-to-church-together" friendship. It indicates a mutual benefit and commitment. In a business enterprise, when people are partners, they are privileged to share the spoils, but they must also share the responsibilities. A friend once said to me, "Everyone wants to cut covenant, but no one wants to bleed." How true!

Relationships are valuable because they are costly. They

cost time and often money. Jesus taught us that our affec-
tions always follow our investments. He said, "Where your
treasure is, there your heart will be also" (Matt. 6:21).

Even in our congregational life, spiritual leaders choose
the level of relationship for their congregations, which
ultimately determine the destiny of that ministry. I believe
that the relationship style a local ministry chooses will
allow that ministry to be one of the following groups: a
gathering, a *tabernacle* or a *city*.

A *gathering* is a group of people who have just come
together under a common banner for the purpose of meeting. When the meeting is over the relationships are over.

On the other hand, a *tabernacle* is a gathering of people
who have blended their hearts together for the purpose of
making a habitation for the presence of the Lord. Their
relationship is driven by the mutual desire to experience
God.

RELATIONSHIPS ARE VALUABLE
BECAUSE THEY ARE COSTLY.
THEY COST TIME
AND OFTEN MONEY.

But the highest order of corporate worship is when the
body of Christ in a local city or nation learns to come
together as a *city*. A *city* is a covenanted community of
believers who have come together for the express purpose
of manifesting the presence of God and exercising govern-
ments. Abraham "looked for a city" (Heb. 11:10, KJV). He
was not looking for Chicago or London—he was looking
for a covenanted group of people who would demonstrate

the kingdom of God on the earth!

If we are going to make a significant impact in our generation, we must be willing to come together in covenant relationships for the express purpose of manifesting God's presence and government. Only when both are joined together do we break the back of the enemy, find a release for the captives and see the revealing of the goodness of God.

Every Joint Supplies

The apostle Paul demonstrates the effect of covenantal relationships through an illustration of the natural body and the power and potential of being properly joined. He writes:

> But, speaking the truth in love, may grow up in all things into Him who is the head—Christ—from whom the whole body, joined and knit together by what every joint supplies, according to the effective working by which every part does its share, causes growth of the body for the edifying of itself in love.
>
> —EPHESIANS 4:15–16

Paul is explaining the process by which the natural body grows and changes. Every bone in your adult body was present in your body when you were a baby, only not as large or as strong as they are now. How did you become the size you are now? At the end of each bone there is a *joint*. The end of each bone has what is commonly known as a "growth plate." The growth plate determines the length and shape of the mature bone. When growth is complete—sometime during adolescence—the growth plates are replaced by solid bone.[1] Life flows through the bone, through the joint into the other bones, causing growth and expansion.

Medical doctors will tell you that dropping a little baby could result in an accident causing damage to the growth plate. If a growth plate is damaged, the child could experience stunted growth in the injured limb or body part.

How valuable it would be for us to realize that we either build ourselves up or tear ourselves down by the relationships that we have in our life. Notice that Paul said, "Every joint supplies." That means that if we get properly connected with brothers and sisters in Christ who nurture our gifts and callings, we can grow to be people we never dreamed possible. However, if we get connected relationally to people who refuse to celebrate our dreams and encourage our walk, we can destroy the very potential that God has put in our hearts.

Be careful! Relationships are powerful. First Corinthians 15:33 declares, "Bad company corrupts good character" (NLT). However, in Proverbs 13:20, the Word declares that if we walk with wise men, we will be wise.

WE EITHER BUILD OURSELVES UP OR TEAR OURSELVES DOWN BY THE RELATIONSHIPS THAT WE HAVE IN OUR LIFE.

Several years ago, an attitude swept throughout the Charismatic movement across the nations that it was not important to be joined to a local church. I understand the hearts of those who promoted such teaching. They were trying to express a sense of liberty to those who had been imprisoned by pious religiosity. But I also recognize the dangers that come to people who never get connected.

There is great benefit to being connected to spiritual brothers and sisters.

> Those who are planted in the house of the LORD
> Shall flourish in the courts of our God.
>
> —PSALM 92:13

Being planted, connected through a root system, is imperative if we are to reach a point of significance in our journey. Far too many believers are constantly being uprooted and moved around. Whether this is happening because of some arising fad or to get to the latest "hot meeting" in town, it is destroying their growth potential.

Proper relationships demand a measure of discernment. When an individual gets planted in the wrong environment or with the wrong people, it limits that person's abilities and gifts. For example, in South Florida there are miles and miles of orange groves. Orange trees flourish here. They produce truckloads of fruit each year. In all the years I lived in South Florida, I walked by hundreds of orange trees. Never once did I ever hear an orange tree straining to produce oranges. Why? It was created to produce oranges. It is in the right environment to produce oranges. It is being nurtured to produce oranges.

However, if you were to take that same orange tree out of South Florida and plant it in Wisconsin, it would be tragic. To survive at all it would need to be a houseplant for part of the year, brought in out of the frigid winters of the cold north. It would demand special attention, continual nurturing and frequent supervision. At best it would produce smaller than normal oranges and become nothing more than a "conversation piece" in the house in which it is being kept.

Here is the question: Is there anything wrong with the orange tree? No. Is there anything wrong with Wisconsin? No. What is the problem? Wrong planting!

The same is true in the life of believers who get involved in relationships that are not ordered by the Lord. There is nothing wrong with their gift. There is nothing wrong with the church or ministry with which they are involved. It is just not the right relationship for them. As a result they become weak, struggling, frustrated believers who demand a lot of attention, continual nurturing and frequent supervision. They end up being the topic of conversation because they are always drawing attention to themselves because of their unhappiness. Or they rebel against the place where they are, declaring that place is not "good soil." No...it's just the wrong soil for their growth potential.

Properly Placed

In Paul's instruction to the church in Corinth concerning order and structure, he said, "But now God has set the members, each one of them, in the body just as He pleased" (1 Cor. 12:18). There are some pretty interesting details in this verse for those who are want to understand the believer's purpose and destiny. The passage makes it clear that we don't really determine our destiny; *we discover it!*

The word *set* is written in a past tense and passive voice. That means that it is something that is done for you. It was prepared before you got there. It was set in place, and then you arrived.

Throughout Scripture we see this biblical principle at work in the lives of God's people. Perhaps the best-known example is in the words God spoke to Jeremiah:

> Before I formed you in the womb I knew you;
> Before you were born I sanctified you;
> I ordained you a prophet to the nations.
>
> —JEREMIAH 1:5

Our purpose and function are determined before we arrive. We don't determine them; we discover them. That is why prayer and counsel are so important in the life of a believer. We are on a journey to significance, and we must discover or discern the place of our anointing and grace.

WE DON'T REALLY DETERMINE OUR DESTINY; WE DISCOVER IT!

You see, the truth is that He sets and we sit. Sitting is something that is active tense and is presently being carried out. Once you discover your place in the body of Christ—the place where He "sets each member as He wills"—then it is your responsibility to sit there. You must take your place in the place of His choosing. When you do that, you properly relate to the rest of the body of Christ. You *fit*, and you *flow*!

If you try to *sit* where He didn't *set* you, then you will be "up-set," and upset everyone else around you. Stop trying to be someone other than whom God has ordained you to be. Your significance does not come from being someone you think is famous or extremely gifted. Your significance comes in finding your place of function in the body of Christ and fulfilling that mandate. Then success will be yours.

David understood that if he was to be success at leading a nation, he could not do it by himself. You can kill
giants alone, but you cannot subdue nations without partnership. So rather than operating as the Lone Ranger of
Israel, David was willing to make covenant relationships.

STOP TRYING TO BE SOMEONE OTHER THAN WHOM GOD HAS ORDAINED YOU TO BE.

In 1 Chronicles 12, David reveals his heart in covenant
making. As the mighty men of Israel gathered before him,
he told them, "If you have come peaceably to me to help
me, my heart will be united with you; but if to betray me
to my enemies, since there is no wrong in my hands, may
the God of our fathers look and bring judgment" (1
Chron. 12:17). As the mighty men gathered to join their
hearts to his, David did what is typical of men making
covenant in that day. First, he would have removed his
weapons belt. Next, he would have removed his robes. He
was defenseless and open before them. His questions for
them become guidelines for us to follow in building
covenant relationships.

"Do you come peaceably?"
David was asking, "Do you come in the spirit you represent here today, or do you have a hidden agenda?" David
needed to know whether they were like those who walk up
smiling, saying all the right things, but concealing hidden
daggers in their hands behind their backs. David was a
mighty warrior, but he made himself vulnerable at that
point for the sake of building trusting relationships.

We have to recognize that it is impossible to build real relationships if we continue to hide behind all the self-protection mechanisms that we have built up in our lives. It may be frightening to become vulnerable, but it is imperative if we are to build lasting relationships.

Ask the questions, evaluate the attitudes, check the motives—but in the end realize that only God can protect you.

"Do you come to help me?"

The heart of this question was directed toward their willingness to celebrate his calling and mandate. He was chosen by God to be king. He could not rule alone, and he wanted those who shared his passion and vision to surround him. He asked the question to determine whether they sincerely wanted to help him fulfill his dream, or whether they came with their own agenda and were seeking his influence to give them a platform from which to launch.

It is easy to take advantage of our opportunities to be close to people of influence and turn them into opportunities for self-gain and self-promotion.

David was well aware that these covenant relationships would become the key to his success. There is a strong indication here that David was a secure man in the fact that he was not making a covenant with weaklings—these were mighty men. So often we only want those people around us who will flatter us with praise. If so, we are failing to realize that we need mighty men and women in our lives if we are to arrive at the destination God has planned for us.

The fact that Hebron was a difficult place to get to geographically gives a spiritual picture to consider. Covenant relationships are so important for each of us, yet so hard to arrive at. There is no question in our minds why Paul, when speaking about spiritual warfare in Ephesians 6, puts all the instruction concerning our struggle in the context of relationships. He has just finished telling husbands and wives how to relate, parents and children how to get along and employers and employees how to respect one another in a business relationship.

From his instruction regarding relationships, he moves directly toward spiritual warfare. Have you ever wondered why he put his teaching about spiritual warfare in the midst of that context? Could it be that he understood something about which we need to have revelation? Relationships are the primary realm of spiritual opposition. We have to learn how to walk in integrity with our brethren, endure the betrayals without bitterness and continue our commitment toward unity if we are to fulfill the commandment of the Lord. We really are built for connection!

An important key is our ability to discern the connections! In the biblical story of Ruth, we discover that her mother-in-law, Naomi, had heard that there was fresh bread in Bethlehem. It was a time of famine in Moab where they lived, and Naomi decided to return to her homeland of Judah. She told her daughters-in-law, Orpah and Ruth, that she was going home. She had lost her husband and sons in Moab, and she was longing to return to the place of her heritage.

Both Orpah and Ruth said they would go with her. However, when Naomi told them that she had nothing to offer them, since she was a widow, Orpah decided she was not going to make the trip. The Bible says, "Orpah kissed her mother-in-law, but Ruth clung to her" (Ruth 1:14).

Orpah kissed, but Ruth clung. That's a picture that depicts many of our relationships today. We have far too many kissers and not enough *clingers*! True covenant relationship moves beyond the realm of "What can you do for me?" It moves into the realm of saying, "I'll go where you go. Your people will be my people. Where you lodge, I will lodge." That is true covenant!

If we are to be people of impact, we must realize we will not do it alone. Relationships are the avenue for God to work His purposes out in our lives. It is "Christ in you" (plural, meaning all of us) that is "the hope of glory"! (See Colossians 1:27.)

chapter nine

The
Process
of Change

For those who were alive a century ago, I am sure they felt that things in their world were changing pretty rapidly. Every few months, new discoveries were being made that affected the American way of life. No doubt they heard people saying things like, "Thomas Edison has made a new discovery called *a light bulb*," or "Those Wright brothers are *flying!*"

For some, the thoughts of change were foolishness—like the men who were determined to resist other emerging modes of transportation because of their firm belief that the railroad system was the supreme method for moving people and products. Or those who believed that there would never be any need for personal computers in our

homes. My grandfather saw such changes in his generation. During his lifetime, transportation progressed from
horse and buggy to putting a man on the moon.

Our world is no different. Landmarks are changing so
rapidly one can hardly determine where he is standing! Just
twenty-five years after the first test-tube baby, we are now
living in a society where it is possible for a woman to give
birth to her own grandchild, people can reproduce children
after they die and a child can have "multiple" parents.
Some of the futurists of our day are predicting that the
majority of the jobs our present high school graduates will
hold during their lifetimes have not even been invented yet!

In all of this, one thing is clear—*change is here to stay!*
We never reach a point in our lives when we are no longer
confronted with the need to change. Everything that is
alive and growing is ever changing.

Sometimes we try to make ourselves believe that we can
arrive at a place of productivity and destiny without making any adjustments. I have heard it said that the defini-
tion of *insanity* is to believe that you can keep doing what
you have been doing and expect to get different results.
When I was an athlete, people used to say, "Practice
makes perfect," but I learned that was not true. Doing
things properly during practice makes one efficient, but
bad habits practiced over and over will never make one
good. There must be a willingness to make corrections.

Change is a choice! That is why it is important for us to
become proactive in the process of change. If not, the
changing times in which we are living will control our lives
for us. *When we fail to be proactive in the arena of change,
we end up being reactive because we were inactive!*

There are several buzzwords resounding throughout

church culture and church leadership today. They are *transition*, *breakthrough* and *new levels*. People are beginning to recognize that *transition* is the beginning process for all advancement in the kingdom. Transition denotes movement. *Breakthrough* is the result of change being implemented. Breakthrough denotes obstacles and barriers that have been overcome. *New levels* are where we find ourselves after the transition and breakthroughs have taken place. New levels denote increased spiritual dynamics and broadened opportunities.

WE NEVER REACH A POINT IN OUR LIVES WHEN WE ARE NO LONGER CONFRONTED WITH THE NEED TO CHANGE.

However, this cycle is not a once-in-a-lifetime event. It is a continual process as we choose the path of personal growth and spiritual maturity. The principles of Scripture teach that *all progress is a process!* We go from:

- "...glory to glory" (2 Cor. 3:18)
- "...faith to faith" (Rom. 1:17)
- "... strength to strength" (Ps. 84:7)

The pathway that you have walked in the past has gotten you to this point, but it may not be able to get you to the next place. God is going to stretch you and expand your horizons. Your journey to significance is not about maintaining the status quo, saying, "My father never made more than $25,000 in a year, so I could never expect to make more than that." Wrong! God is going to blow the roof off. The ceilings of limitation and containment that have been on your life are coming off. Just as David moved from shepherd boy to valiant warrior to national hero to king, we too must take the initiative to embrace the new! Our pathway has been prepared by Him, but He requires our cooperation. Get out of the rut. Break free from the rigidity of old wineskins. Stop saying, "That's just always how I have done it."

CHANGE MUST BE FOUNDED IN PURPOSE AND VISION!

Routine alone is not our problem. We can't live with it; we can't live without it. Established procedures annoy us, yet we all expect airplanes and trains to run on time. Repetition is a tedious way to work. Who could ever forget the television advertisement "It's time to make the dough-nuts"? Yet, if we never did anything the same way twice, how would we ever be able to develop manufacturing pro-cedures, get returns on our initial investments or fine-tune the quality of the things we produce? It might be routine, but the doughnut man makes doughnuts every day—and makes them of a consistent quality!

That is why we must understand that when we change just to change, we create more problems than we solve. Change must be founded in purpose and vision! We have to be *seeing* something more than what we have at the moment.

When I was a small boy, my schoolteacher sent a note home to my mother asking her to teach me how to color. She stated in the note that it was important that I learn to color properly and neatly. It seems that I colored all over the page.

My mother asked me to color a picture for her. Sure

enough, the marks of the crayon were all over the page. Mom sat me down and said, "Son, I know you are enjoying your coloring, but you have to learn to color the picture that is on the page and to stay inside the lines."

I remember asking my mother, "Who said that a house has to look like that picture? Why can't it look like I drew it?" She just laughed.

Many years later, God entrusted me with the leadership of a ministry. One day in a staff meeting we were discussing an issue that demanded creative, bold thinking. While we were talking, I suddenly remembered that day as a child. At that moment I realized that our environment teaches us to conform and to play it safe rather than to be bold and innovative. That day I told my staff, "It is time for us to color outside the lines!"

The answer to your dilemma could be hidden in your willingness to do something radical and outside the box. Your willingness to let go of the old is an indication of what God can bring to you. Your future is in your present. How often have you heard someone say, "God is doing a new thing," and you agree, only to realize later that what was said and what you heard were entirely different things? What you heard was "...new thing." What you expected was "...the same ole' stuff!"

One of the most frustrating things in life is when we gain a new revelation or experience and try to fit it into an old habit!

How often have you missed divine opportunities to make progress and to experience a breakthrough because you responded as a creature of habit? Most of us go the same way to work every day, sit in the same seat in church and eat the same breakfast every morning. But an invitation is being given us to get on a new road:

> Behold, I am doing a new thing!...do you not per-
> ceive and know it?

> —ISAIAH 43:19, AMP

There are many reasons why people fear change. I have found that many people are in love with the *image* of success, but they are far less interested in the *process* of becoming successful. To become successful, you must be willing to embrace the process of change, even if it demands overcoming the fear that has held you captive.

There are several reasons why we resist change. Let's take a closer look at these reasons.

The Unknown

I am sure you have heard this saying: "People are usually down on what they are not up on." Change demands that you be willing to move into new areas that may be unfamiliar to you. While change is not based on "blind faith," which is neither biblical nor wise, it does put us in the uncomfortable position of not knowing its results up-front. I have to be willing to leave the shoreline of safe, predictable living and launch out into new arenas of function and thinking. A true change agent possesses the willingness to move into uncharted territory for the sake of greater productivity and efficiency. David had never killed a giant. No one in Israel had ever killed a giant that we know of. But David knew that the nation could not stay where it was— hiding in fear and intimidation—so he "colored outside the lines" and ran to battle!

For God has not given us a spirit of timidity, but of power and love and discipline.

—2 TIMOTHY 1:7, NAS

Resist the insecurities that keep holding you back. Let go of being so image conscious that you always have to look as if you know exactly what you are doing. Abraham let go! He "obeyed when he was called to go out to the place which he would receive as an inheritance. And he went out, not knowing where he was going" (Heb. 11:8).

GOD WILL ALWAYS ANOINT YOU TO THE LEVEL OF YOUR FAITH! THE UNKNOWN IS NOT IMPOSSIBLE, JUST UNKNOWN!

We must follow Abraham's example of obedience. It is more important for you to respond in obedience and to launch out than it is to have all the understanding of how your decision is going to work out. Hudson Taylor had no idea how he would be received in China, but he went anyway. Queen Esther did not know if the king would hear her or kill her, but she asked to see him anyway. Determine to act with confidence. God is attracted to your faith! "Without faith it is impossible to please [God]" (Heb. 11:6).

God will never give you a life where faith is not necessary. Who told you that it could not be done? Who told you that you could not own a home or get the job? God will always anoint you to the level of your faith! The unknown is not impossible, just unknown!

The Risk Factor

Change is not possible without taking risks. When David confronted Goliath, there was a possibility that he would be killed. Don't misunderstand me; he was acting in faith. Fear was not controlling his life. Nevertheless, there was a risk involved in running toward a giant! Victory only really becomes sweet in our lives when there was a possibility of defeat.

We are consumed with football in our nation from August through January. I have noticed that there are varying degrees of enthusiasm at differing points of the season. In August, the NFL has what is known as "pre-season." It is a time for practicing new plays, looking at new players and getting in shape. The veterans play only a portion of the game, and everyone plays carefully, not wanting to get hurt before the season opens. Every player wants to be healthy for the "regular season." Because it is preseason, no one really celebrates the victories, nor do they feel badly about the losses. Why? The games don't count! There is no risk to losing!

Once the regular season begins, everything is different. The energy levels, the strategic planning, the willingness to play hurt, the motivation—all of it rises to a new level. Why? It counts! To lose during the regular season is to risk missing the playoffs and a championship.

The same is true in the life of a believer. Far too often we think of life as just a preseason, and we play to not get hurt. Instead of using all our energy and motivation to accomplish what God is saying to us, we go through the motions of pursuing destiny. But when there is no risk factor to our walk with God, there will be very little celebration in our lives. We will miss the opportunity to play for the championship and become world changers.

You may have to put it all on the line. It may be that God has been speaking to you about starting your own business, and you have been trying to play it safe. Maybe there is a call on your life for ministry, and you are hesitant to respond because it means risking dreams, finances or relationships. You will never change without taking the risk necessary to process that change.

The Force of Environment

The writer of Hebrews speaks of the time when those who followed after the purposes of God in their lives did not spend time thinking about *where they came from*. If they had, they would have returned to that place (Heb. 11:15). The environment in which you presently live, or the one in which you grew up, can become a powerful force that hinders change in your life. We often reject anything that is different than we are. Friends and family may help us progress—but they can also hinder our progress. Many people are locked up in frustrated living because they allowed the sentimental feelings of family members to manipulate them into making decisions that caused them to forfeit their destinies.

I have a friend whose name is Paul. He is a pastor from Poland. Having grown up under the domination of Communism where he learned the difficulties of life firsthand, it was easy for him to develop constrictive thinking. During several of his adolescent years, Paul had to stand in line for six hours a day to get two loaves of bread and half a gallon of milk. His family was apportioned four pounds of meat per month. Soup became the main course for many meals.

After he married and had children, Paul once stood in line for two weeks, never leaving the line for a single day, in order to purchase a washing machine. When he finally reached the front of the line, he was told that no more washing machines would be available for two more weeks. However, he was told, "We have three refrigerators." He was third in line. Two weeks earlier he came for a washing machine, but he went home with a refrigerator. That was all that was available to him.

After he was born again through the Catholic Charismatic movement in Poland, Paul knew God had called him to preach the gospel. He began a church in the north of the country with just a few people. Although his congregation was small, his heart was reaching for something more. He began to dream about facilities, multimedia ministry, music teams and hosting conferences. His faith grew, and supernaturally, God began to supply his needs.

One day while visiting in London, he was speaking with a pastor concerning the vision of his ministry and what he believed God wanted to do. In the midst of the conversation, the pastor from London stopped Paul and said to him, "You are thinking Polish!" It startled Paul. In fact, it was quite flabbergasting to him!

Why would he say that to me? Paul asked to himself. Then he asked the pastor to explain what he meant.

"God has not left Poland, Paul," the pastor told him. "The same God who has opened all the doors for you up to this point, supernaturally supplying what you have needed to walk through them, is still with you. There are no limits to what you can do."

At that point, Paul's eyes (and mind) were opened! He realized that he was viewing God from the context of his environment rather than from the power of God's promises. Paul was radically changed. Today he pastors one of the leading churches in the nation and has influence with people throughout Poland. His vision is bigger than ever, and he has exceeded every standard for "church life" in his nation.

How could that happen? Simple. He refused to allow the force of his environment to keep him from instituting change!

Our environment—family traditions, cultural barriers, economic depression, neighborhood history, wrong relationships—has a tremendous force over our lives if we keep our minds stayed on it. If you keep thinking about where you came from, longing for it with affection, it will be very easy to go back there and find yourself in a limited world.

The Instant Success Syndrome

We live in a society that enjoys things that are fast. We like "microwave living"! Quick and easy...no mess. However, life is not that way. It is often quite the opposite. Some quit after three days if there is no sign of success! For the people recorded in history as people who changed the course of a nation, city or family, the rewards of their obedience often came slowly or even after their death.

The only reason we endure the process of change is because we see something different at the end of our waiting.

These all died in faith, not having received the promises, but having seen them afar off...

—HEBREWS 11:13

Write the vision...Though it tarries, wait for it; because it will surely come, it will not tarry.

—HABAKKUK 2:2–3

Looking unto Jesus, the author and finisher of our faith, who for the joy that was set before Him endured the cross.

—HEBREWS 12:2

Let us not grow weary while doing good, for in due season we shall reap if we do not lose heart.

—GALATIANS 6:9

Throughout his entire life, Abraham walked by faith, looking for something he never fully received. But his seed, and his seed's seed, did receive it!

THERE IS NO SUCCESS WITHOUT SACRIFICE!

The changes that happen to you are not just for your own comfort and convenience. Rather they are for the generations that are coming after you. By your willingness to endure the process, many people will experience a world different from the one we inherited from our fathers.

I am grateful today that my children have not had to grow up in the hatred and bitterness of the Civil Rights movement of the sixties. Dr. Martin L. King Jr. never really saw the things he dreamed about come to pass. However, we are the recipients of the courage and conviction that drove him to speak out for change.

Our church does not struggle over its identity as a full-gospel congregation of believers who practice expressive worship and believe in the manifestations of the Holy Spirit. We freely exercise spiritual language and pray for the sick. The reason we don't have that struggle today is because there was a band of sold-out believers in our city in 1939 that took a stand for change. They believed that our city needed a full gospel church. From those small beginnings, today many of our city leaders are bold, vibrant Christians.

There is no success without sacrifice! If you are enjoying a measure of success today, it is only because someone went before you and paved the way through their endurance and conviction. Let's be thankful for those on whose shoulders we stand!

If you are sacrificing and not experiencing an immediate return, then rejoice. You are paving the way for someone who is coming after you. You may never see the fruit of your efforts to initiate change, but those for whom you open the door will inherit the promise and much more.

The Stages of Processing Change

Change demands process. In our discovery of the process of change, it is important to note that every level of change has an increasing degree of difficulty and a greater length of time. Some things can be changed in an hour; others take years. Some are not so hard to accomplish, while others are painful and demanding. In this section we are going to take a look at the process of change as it takes place within our lives.

In the graph below, we show the process of change and how it works out in our lives. The higher up vertically on the scale you go, the more difficult it will be to implement change. The further out horizontally on the scale you go, the more time it will take to bring about the change desired.

The Stages of Change

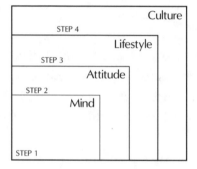

At each stage on the chart, we will need to learn now to process change. Let's see how we do that at each stage.

Step 1—*Your mind*

The quickest and easiest thing to change is your mind. Most of us change our minds several times in the course of just one day. If you find that hard to believe, you are probably not married!

Your ability to make adjustments in your thinking is the cornerstone to processing change in your life. If you can change your mind, you can change anything. However, if

you cannot change your mind, you will find it very difficult to facilitate change in any area of your life. George
Bernard Shaw once said, "Progress is impossible without
change; and those who cannot change their minds cannot
change anything."

I have found that the necessary ingredient in changing
your mind is *information*. Your decision making can only
be as good as the information you have available to you at
the time of the decision. That is why it becomes easy to
change your decision when more information has become
available.

One of my daughters came home from school one afternoon and asked to spend the night with a friend. We knew
the family and agreed to let her go. A little later that day,
my wife was in the grocery store and saw the mother of
the young lady with whom we had given permission for
our daughter to spend the night. As my wife and the girl's
mother were talking together, the mother told my wife that
she and her husband were leaving later that day for a trip.
Remembering that our daughter had asked to spend that
night with her friend, my wife asked, "Will you and your
husband be home tonight when my daughter comes to
spend the night?"

"No," she replied. "My husband and I are leaving, and
the girls are staying by themselves."

When my wife arrived back home and shared the information she had obtained while at the grocery store, I called
my daughter into the kitchen and told her, "You will not
be permitted to stay over at your friend's house tonight."
Of course, that was not received real well.

As she bemoaned her sudden change of plans, she said,
"See, you are always subject to change your mind. It is not

fair. I don't know what to expect."

I responded to her, "You are right. I am subject to change my mind, especially when more information becomes available to me. I found out your friend's parents are not going to be at home." At that point, she knew I had the information I needed for the decision of whether she could spend the night away.

In the body of Christ, often we live in ignorance of the truth because we fail to pursue the information necessary to embrace a life of change. Satan does not want you to have all the information available to you. He wants to convince you that the habits and limitations present in your life are permanent and that there is nothing you can do to make them any different. As long as you accept his word as fact, you will live a life of frustration and bondage.

The prophet Hosea declared that people were being cut off from their potential and destiny because of their lack of awareness and understanding.

> My people are destroyed for lack of knowledge.
>
> —HOSEA 4:6

It has been said that *what you don't know won't hurt you.* But in the kingdom of God, what you don't know may kill you! It is imperative that you obtain the information you need to make godly decisions in your life.

> Through wisdom a house is built,
> And by understanding it is established;
> By knowledge the rooms are filled
> With all precious and pleasant riches.
>
> —PROVERBS 24:3–4

I heard the late John Osteen, former pastor of Lakewood

Church in Houston, Texas, make this statement one day: "When you leave the meeting today, you will need more than inspiration; you will need information. It is the information that you have that will enable you to overcome the attacks of the enemy when the inspiration has left." How true that is. When the worship team is no longer singing and the encouragers have all gone home, it is the truth that you know that will set you free.

The Holy Spirit illuminates information to give revelation. *Revelation*, which is truth that has been become revealed or uncovered, is the initiator of transformation. And *transformation* is the avenue for *manifestation!* If we are going to see the large-scale manifestation of God's glory in the earth, we must begin by getting people the proper information.

When a man who has spent the last ten years of his life bound by crack cocaine finds out that he can be free, that information is the catalyst that launches him into the process of change. His changed life and new character become a visible sign, or a manifestation, that God has done a work in his life. By his testimony, God is glorified.

The key to obtaining good information is the willingness to hear. Some people only want to hear information from those in their own church or denominational group. Some refuse to receive insight or wisdom from anyone who is not just like them. By resisting "cross-pollination," we create an environment for birthing deformed truths. It is like buying a puppy from a pet store and discovering the puppy has hip dysplasia as the result of being interbred for too many generations. By cross-pollination we avoid the problems created by drawing only from the same gene pool.

Since our thinking has a tremendous bearing on our performance, our thinking must be based on sound principles and truth. In order to think right, we have to pursue the proper information. We were given a mind so that we could gather information and comprehend truth. Once that is done, we are better suited for making decisions based on sound judgment.

The challenge in the twenty-first century church is being willing to embrace truth even when it comes from outside your *camp*. The information you receive will aid in the process of changing your mind. When church leaders refuse to pursue truth simply because it comes in different packaging, they are sentencing those under their leadership to limitations. Eventually they will birth doctrines and practices that are destructive.

Step 2—Your attitude

```
                        Attitude
        STEP 2
                    Mind

        STEP 1
```

After changing your mind, the next most difficult thing to change is your *attitude*. Our attitude is the expression of our inner man. That part of our life—the mind, will and emotions—becomes the avenue for releasing the spirit man. The longer I live the more I realize the impact of attitude on our lives. To me, attitude is more important than facts. It is more important than the past, money, education, our successes or failures, the circumstances that surround us or even the things people say about us. It is more forceful than our appearance, gifted abilities or skills in affecting the lives of others.

Attitude is vital. It is the difference between winning and losing, success and failure. There are many things that are important in your personal development and journey to significance, but without proper attitudinal development you will stifle your potential and close doors of opportunity that could have been roadways to accomplishment. Every day you make a choice about the attitude you will embrace for that day. Much of what you face each day you cannot control or change. The one thing you can do is guard your attitude!

Charles Swindoll has said, "I am convinced that life is 10 percent what happens to me and 90 percent how I react to it."

Many times in our leadership development seminars, I conduct an "unscientific" survey. While not totally definitive, it is a revealer of truth. I ask the attendees to do the following: "Think of the people in life you most respect and admire. Now tell me the qualities those people possess that you most want to emulate in your life." I then begin to write the answers on a white board. The answers always include characteristics such as perseverance, humility, joyfulness, trustworthiness, courage and faithfulness.

When we finish listing all the qualities, I then write three letters on the top of the board—"S" for skills, "L" for looks and "A" for attitude. Then I designate each response with one of the letters. The results have been amazing. Whether we are in North America, Europe, Africa or the South Pacific, the survey comes out the same. More than 90 percent of the responses have the letter "A" beside them, denoting attitude as the thing people most want to follow. Hardly ever do we get an "S" or an "L."

This is an indicator of how important attitude is. Attitude moves people. Yet, how many people will spend thousands of dollars developing their skills or thousands of hours improving their looks, but nothing improving their attitude? It is not our Armani suits or Gucci purses that people are after. They want the ability to change their attitudes in order to change their world.

"I AM CONVINCED THAT LIFE IS 10 PERCENT WHAT HAPPENS TO ME AND 90 PERCENT HOW I REACT TO IT."

The first time we hear new truth that challenges our thinking or actions we are probably not happy campers. Truth can often upset us before it blesses us. Many times we react negatively to the one who confronts us with the need for change. That is why we must be committed to the relationship until we can process the change. Maintaining committed relationships is a key factor to your ability to process change in the arena of your attitude.

During the mentoring process, it has often been necessary for me to confront people with truth they needed to hear in order to fulfill their destinies and to change their lives. Sometimes the people will rejoice at hearing the truth, but many have reacted negatively. I do not allow their negative reactions to push me away from relationship with them. Instead, I reaffirm my commitment to each individual, affirming that I am committed to them through the duration of the process. As a result, we are able to work through the issues together.

A married couple who recognizes the need for change in their marriage, yet unwilling to be committed to the relationship while that change is being processed, may damage or lose their marriage. The level of commitment often dictates the probability of positive change. Attitudinal changes take place in the heart—the place where relationships begin.

Step 3—Your lifestyle

```
                        Lifestyle
        STEP 3
                   Attitude
        STEP 2
            Mind

    STEP 1
```

Lifestyle changes are not made without changing your mind and your attitudes. Lifestyles change when embraced truth becomes a way of life.

Leonard Sweet has said, "Faith in God is dangerous thinking. Even more, faith in God is dangerous living."[1] Life in Christ is not just about keeping rules and quoting doctrines. That was the mistake the Pharisees made. They believed keeping a regimen of sacred order would somehow result in a life of righteousness. But true lifestyle changes are the result of intimate relationship on an *experiential level*.

> And you shall know the truth, and the truth shall make you free.
>
> —JOHN 8:32

To *know the truth* means to have intimate interaction

with truth. It is not just truth that has been memorized or written on a "daily promise card." Rather it is truth that has been wrestled with, held tightly and fully embraced. That intimate knowledge, as when Adam knew his wife and she bare him a son, is what makes us free. In order to have a lifestyle change, you must have *experiences and exposure!* Some things are better *caught* than *taught.*

The only way the world is going to see the glory of God is through believers who are manifesting the truth of God's Word in their flesh...in their lifestyles!

To learn how to be a worshiper, you must spend time with those who really understand the ways of worship and have a heart to worship. The truth that has liberated them will be experienced while you worship with them, and it will become a part of your spirit. If you want to know how to live a clean, pure life, find people who have learned to "walk out truth," and stay with them. Don't waste your time hanging around with those who have no respect for your devotion to the Lord and no desire to have a heart that is upright before the Lord.

When your lifestyle begins to change, the world will begin to see truth through you. The Word declares:

> The Word became flesh, and dwelt among us, and we beheld His glory, glory as of the only begotten

from the Father, full of grace and truth.

—JOHN 1:14, NAS

The only way the world is going to see the glory of God is through believers who are manifesting the truth of God's Word in their flesh...in their lifestyles! We must be committed to moving truth from the realm of theory to practice. The truth that will change our lives and our world has the ability to get down in the dirt of life and do its work. What we know as truth must become a part of our way of living if we are going to usher kingdom dynamics into the generation we have been called to impact.

Step 4—Your culture

```
                                          Culture
            STEP 4
                               Lifestyle
          STEP 3
                        Attitude
        STEP 2
                   Mind
    STEP 1
```

The end result of the process of change is that your life will have a genuine affect upon our culture. You will become the "salt of the earth"!

Most sociologists believe that it takes five to seven years to bring change to established culture. Culture, like a large ship, does not change direction quickly. Our media industry in America understands that concept. For many years, we have seen the subtle inclusion of what was once seen as cultural taboos being added to the scripts of sitcoms and theater. What my grandparents would have considered vulgar and offensive is normal nightly television in our

culture. How did it happen? It started with a war on our
thinking. After the initial outrage, our attitudes became
accepting, and from there, lifestyles emerged from "the
closet." Today, many of our earlier cultural taboos are
accepted as a way of life.

As a believer, you must understand that you can change
your sphere of influence if you are willing to master the
process. You cannot expect a quick return on a long-term
lifestyle investment. You have heard it said, "Well, you
can't change the world!" Right! But you do have the ability to change your spot in the world. If enough spots are
changed, then the world will be affected, and your journey
will take on new meaning and significance.

It disturbs me when I see Christians attack our culture
with the false assumption that they can initiate change
through that attack. Merely attacking it never changes culture. It is a waste of energy and resources to point accus-
ing fingers at political figures and bemoan the decisions of
the courts in our land without offering any new information to those who are searching for direction.

Many of the people caught in the trap of bondage, disappointment and despair are not happy about their lot in
life. They just don't know the way out! How often have
you heard a third-grade child say, "When I grow up, I
want to a crack addict"? Or what fifth-grade little girl says,
"When I am sixteen, I want to be single mother living on
the street and having to sell my body to feed my baby"?

Never! So how do bondages get broken and lives get
set free? How does a young man who wanted the love of
a father who was never home get out of the grip of
homosexuality? How does a woman who desires a husband who will love and honor her deal with a fantasy

world created by a craving for romance novels and afternoon soap operas? Is there any way out?

Yes! It happens through the process of change! It takes information...caring relationships...experiences with truth...and the time necessary to process it all.

Don't wait any longer. Jesus Christ is offering you a life that overflows! Whether the change you need is in your personal life, your job or your place of ministry, remember this—change begins in you.

chapter ten

The Price of Greatness

N o one will ever water your dreams as well as you do! For those who are satisfied to walk in mediocrity, the highway of life has always been paved with good intentions. "One day I'm gonna..." "Someday soon I believe I will..." "Sometime..." They all become the empty words of people who refuse to grasp the moments that are before them.

Many of those very same people, at an earlier stage in their life, had a desire to make a lasting impact on their generation. They wanted to do something significant, to somehow break free from the rat race of just going to work and coming home. They had goals they really wanted to achieve, goals that had been laid out in front of them by divine providence. Now, for various reasons, those dreams are only faint memories. Maybe it was an unexpected crisis that drained them of their passion or the lack of perception to see the opportunity before them that caused them to grow weary.

For most, the dreams of a lifetime are not lost due to unbearable circumstances or the rejection of those close friends who failed to recognize our potential. Rather, it is our unwillingness to accept the basic foundational truth that we must take responsibility for the life that has been entrusted to us by God. Sir Winston Churchill once said, "The price of greatness is responsibility."[1]

Is it possible that a generation of good people who love God has failed to realize the potential that God has given them because of our "escapism theology"? For most, church life consists of "showing up" and "looking up."

In my childhood we were told that the Antichrist was soon to appear, so don't worry about getting an education, buying property, making wise investments or participating in the dialogue of how to shape our world. The thought of still being on Planet Earth at the turn of the twenty-first century was a fantasy useful only in novels and movies. Now, here we are! We find ourselves in the early stages of a new millennium, scrambling to catch up and be relevant.

"THE PRICE OF GREATNESS IS RESPONSIBILITY."

Our world is pulsating with the pressures of blended marriages, single parenthood, holy wars, the Internet explosion and the globalization of business and government. We must stop allowing our adversary to paralyze us with indifference and status quo thinking.

The devil knows that many Christians will never go back to the world, so he develops a strategy of containment, neutralizing them with the satisfaction of being "bound for heaven"! May I submit to you that getting people to heaven has never been God's dilemma—He can do that with ease. Ask Elijah or Enoch. However, the challenge that has been waged since the conflict in the Garden of Eden is, "How do we get God back in the earth?"

Sure, Christ is going to return to the earth and receive His people. That will be a grand and glorious day. *But what will we do until then?* Who knows but that you were born for such a time as this?

There is a generation arising that refuses to march to the drumbeat of dead, ineffective and irrelevant religiosity. These modern-day "soldiers" are determined that they will not be overtaken with the materialism of previous generations. They will not live just to "make money." The cry of their heart is, "I want to make my world different!" They have watched their parents, grandparents and even great-grandparents survive and overcome the greatest threats in the history of mankind during two world wars. Having grown up in the turbulent times of the demise of communism, fanatical occultism and the rise of radical *jihads*, they are focused on something more than self.

Don't believe what you have been told about a whole generation that many have discounted as being disinterested and bored with church. The scoffers may be right about their disinterest and mockery of much of our organized religion, which seeks self-preservation at the expense of present-day truth. While this generation looks for a purpose worth giving their life to, many others of previous days are busy purposefully giving their time, energy and resources to things that will never bring an eternal impact to them personally or in their world.

Behind all the radical appearances of piercing and tattoos, behind the violent world portrayed in the words of urban rappers and the fantasy land of egotistical princesses who seek to manipulate a generation with their hips and lips, is an emerging generation willing to answer the call to greatness. Their battlefields may be quite different. Much like David, they are out of sight tending to some menial task or preliminary function.

They do not carry protest placards or march on city hall, but they are learning to overcome the jeers of teachers and fellow classmates and the seducing call of a media bent on self-gratification. They are learning to defeat bears and lions that would attempt to destroy their hopes of destiny. They are from every social strata of our world. Some of the most powerful change agents of our generation are coming from the ethnic groups that have been overlooked, considered Third World and forgotten. There are men and women who have left their careers to answer the call. Some are choosing to forsake the road to wealth and comfort in order to accept the invitation to be a world changer and history maker! Some are teenagers who have an intense desire...a passion...to be people who make a significant contribution in this generation.

How can we ever forget the day when some teenagers in a middle-class neighborhood school in Colorado changed the landscape of America with their uncompromising heroism? Who would have ever thought that the challenge to make a difference with your life would be issued with the price of blood?

Rachel Scott did not realize how far her love for Jesus would be felt. On March 1, 1998 she wrote in her journal, "I want heads to turn in the halls when I walk by. I want them to stare at me, watching and wanting the light you have put in me. I want you to overflow my cup with your Spirit...I want you to use me to reach the unreached." On May 2, 1998, she wrote, "This will be my last year, Lord. I have gotten what I can. Thank you."[2]

Rachel's insights proved to be prophetic. She was gunned down for her faith in the Columbine massacre on April 20, 1999. However, heads have turned, and she did reach the unreached. Her life lives on; she touched the place of greatness.

Responsibility Demands Your Attention

I have been blessed with a wonderful wife, three lovely daughters, a son-in-law and a granddaughter. Although there have been days when I wanted to be free to go and do as I pleased without any thought of what was being expected of me, I have had to grow up and learn that I cannot have both. It is not possible for me to have a family who loves me, needs me and for which I am responsible, and to have a carefree lifestyle that has no boundaries, focus or commitments. The same is true for your destiny! The destiny that is before you requires your conscientious cooperation and effort. The secret to success is not in your ability to just say *yes*, but in your ability to say *no*!

There is also a fact of life that you cannot ignore: The more you have, the more you are responsible for. Jesus said, "To whom much is given, from him much will be required" (Luke 12:48). People who don't own a house don't have to worry about repairs and upkeep. Those without a car don't have to worry about buying gas. But with every blessing comes additional responsibility.

Responsibility is the measuring rod for maturity! Maturity is not measured by gray hair and longevity of life. It is measured by a man or woman who has learned to become responsible for himself or herself—and the future. During the years that I have traveled through the nations, I have watched young men and women who were wonderfully gifted with lots of talent and personality, but who did so little with their lives. I've watched musicians who could have been used mightily in worship end up on the sidelines, ineffective and frustrated and wanting to blame everyone else for their lack of success. The truth is, they wanted position, fame and the rewards of success without the price of responsibility.

God's Secret

In Genesis 2 we find a secret to God's plan for mankind. The beginning of the chapter recaps the fact that God created the heavens and the earth. God is the Creator. That separates Him from mankind because, at best, man is only creative. The difference between a creator and someone who is creative is very simple. Someone who is creative still has to have something from which to make something. If an architect wants to make an office building, he must have concrete, steel and wood. If an engineer wants to make a new car, he must have steel for the frame, leather for the seats and rubber for the tires. Materials are needed in order for creative people to manifest their creativity.

But for the Creator, it is different. When there was nothing in existence, God stepped out into eternity past and took nothing and made it into something. He flung it out into nowhere and told it to stay there, and it has been upheld by the power of His word ever since! That is the power of a creator!

RESPONSIBILITY IS THE MEASURING ROD FOR MATURITY!

That is why God did not consult your résumé before He called you to the destiny He has for you. He specializes in taking nobodies and making somebodies out of them. It is not what you bring to the table that makes you a potential world changer. All of our righteousness is but filthy rags. All of our wisdom is silenced in His presence. All of our might fades in the light of His omnipotent power. It is what He, by His grace working in us, will make us to be.

> The LORD God made the earth and the heavens, before any plant of the field was in the earth and before any herb of the field had grown. For the LORD God had not caused it to rain on the earth, and *there was no man to till the ground.*
> —GENESIS 2:4–5, EMPHASIS ADDED

In the Bible account of the genesis of the earth, the writer tells us that there were plants that had sprouted on the earth. Obviously, there were seeds in the ground, but they had not germinated and begun to produce fruit. They were lying dormant in the earth. Future harvest was resident inside those seeds; beautiful blossoms were there too, but no evidence was seen on the earth. Why? There was "no man to till [care for] the ground."

This truth is vitally important to your journey: God never waters "seeds" when He has no man who will take responsibility for them. No man…no sprouts!

What a reality this is in your life! God plants "dream seeds"—seeds of potential, excellence, vision—on the inside of your life. Resident within your spiritual DNA is the purpose of God for your life, with all its accompanying grace and gifting in seed form. But God will not *rain on the seeds* until He sees your willingness to take responsibility for them.

GREATNESS DOES NOT COME PREPACKAGED! IT IS THE RESULT OF HARD WORK, DIFFICULT CHOICES AND A LIFETIME OF GIVING.

Thus, the proverbial axiom, "Are leaders born or made?" Is greatness the result of preordained choosing or disciplined pursuit? Yes! It is both! You may have midwives help you birth a dream, but it has to come through your loins if it is going to have great effectiveness.

God puts abilities within you by creative design. Some of these grace gifts are evident early in your life through the avenue of personality. But others do not manifest until you begin the pursuit of your purpose. No matter what you see now, or what may be emerging through your nudging on the doors of opportunity before you, without the diligence of proper stewardship these grace gifts will end up dormant and unfruitful. That is why the greatest talent pool, the greatest songs ever heard, the best architectural designs ever known and the most awe-inspiring books are never viewed and heard by the multitudes of people they were meant for. Instead, they are lying dormant in a graveyard, having never been rained on!

Greatness does not come prepackaged! It is the result of hard work, difficult choices and a lifetime of giving. You may feel as though you have the world by the tail, or you may feel as out of place as a turtle in a road race. Regardless of how you feel, recognize that your ability to leave behind a legacy of fruitful living is being determined by your willingness to take what has been given to you and, through responsible stewardship, make your world different. To complete your journey to significance, you must realize that *you are an owner of nothing and a manager (steward) of everything.*

You may never be an Abraham Lincoln, a Rachel Scott or a Nelson Mandela. That may not have been in God's plan for your life. But you were meant to steward properly the investment that God has made in you and to produce something that is of profit.

> And the LORD God formed man of the dust of the ground, and breathed into his nostrils the breath of life; and man became a living being. The LORD God planted a garden...there He put the man whom He had formed.
>
> —GENESIS 2:7–8

The word for *formed* is the Hebrew word *yatsar*. It is used to describe something that is molded into shape or form. It could be described to be like what a potter, working with clay, shapes and fashions out of the clay as he determines the use of the vessel he is forming. Adam was not just thrown together as an afterthought in the mind of God. He was fashioned as a steward of God's creation. Once God had a man that could take responsibility for His creation, He planted a garden.

Consumer or Producer?

The original command to mankind was to be fruitful and multiply, subdue your enemies and have dominion upon the earth. By divine intention, God's heart desired for man to be a producer!

Our culture has shaped us into being brilliant consumers. Our retail markets have learned how to grasp the desires of those who drive the markets. We have become accustomed to *being served* rather than being servants!

GOD'S DELIGHT AND OUR FULFILLMENT COME WHEN WE LIVE A LIFE OF PRODUCTIVITY!

We "shop" for a church that our family can be a part of, hardly basing our decisions on the will of God or on being properly planted. We choose our church according to taste and preferences. Sunday has become a time to "shop" for a place where we can get a blessing and receive a word from the Lord—not be a blessing and help someone else make it through! How easy it has become for us to consume with no thought of producing. We must awaken to our God-given potential and change our mind-set! We were born to produce!

> You did not choose Me, but I chose you and
> appointed you that you should go and bear fruit,
> and that your fruit should remain.
>
> —JOHN 15:16

God's delight and our fulfillment come when we live a life of productivity!

The Garden of Eden contained everything that man would ever need to be sustained and fulfilled. His only responsibility was to cultivate it and keep it (Gen. 2:15). From this account we learn several key principles to becoming successful stewards.

We are managers of everything and owners of nothing.

Our entire life is one of stewardship. Whether it is your abilities, your marriage, your children, your job, the opportunities before you for success, your influence—whatever it may be that has been entrusted to you—proper management will determine your success.

Mismanagement always brings separation, guilt and loss.

When Adam failed to *nurture and keep* his garden properly, his ineffective guardianship resulted in the loss of his stewardship of the garden and its resourcefulness. He reaped the guilt born of his disobedience and separation from his place of fellowship with God. He lost the authority such a relationship affords. God came walking in the cool of the day, but something had changed in Adam. God asked the question, "Adam, where are you?" That was not an inquiry about geography, but rather a probing question of positioning and confidence. Adam had never hidden from God before. Adam had never been embarrassed before. But now he was both. Shame had begun to enter his life for the first time. Something was missing!

When we are overtaken by failure or sin, we often attempt to hide from God by covering our exposed weaknesses with imaginary fig leaves. Thinking our fig leaves are "covering the shame," we fail to face up to the reality of mismanagement. When that happens, it is inevitable that the same pattern of Adam's life will be repeated in ours. The pattern goes like this—first we seek to hide from God; then we arrange a cover-up with fig leaves.

Then, when confronted with the truth concerning our actions, we seek to hide behind all kinds of defense mechanisms—anger, moods, spirituality, pride, justifications— and cover up the real problem. Once God "finds" us and begins to inquire as to why we are there, we often respond as victims. Rather than taking the responsibility for what has happened, we seek to shift the blame to someone or something else. In the end, we must finally face our own actions and the consequences for not safeguarding what has been given to us.

You can never transfer responsibility for mismanagement.
We are each responsible before God for our own garden. Never will God allow us to spend our lives blaming someone else for why we are like we are. While many people have been maligned, abused and mistreated, we can never allow our misfortune to become an excuse for our failure to seize our opportunities and potential. It isn't my wife, my job, the city I live in or the church I attend that is to blame. Adam tried to blame Eve. Eve blamed the serpent. The patterns are the same today. Many people seek to transfer responsibility for their own lives to their partners, the government

or the church where they worship.

You must be ever aware that you do not lack the tools to overcome your difficulties. You have the Holy Spirit—and His endless supply of power—available to you in every situation of life. The Word of God must become a source of wisdom and direction for every step of your journey.

The empowerment to get up after failure is available to those who believe!

I learned a long time ago that the difference between great men and average men is not in whether they fall down. Every person at some point in life has failed to steward the potential that God has given and missed the mark. The difference between the two is that great men get back up! If the conditions of your life can cloud your mind, then the devil can make you believe that you are too far-gone and can never recover! The devil is a liar!

> What then shall we say to these things? If God be for us, who can be against us?
>
> —ROMANS 8:31

The apostle Paul is telling you that there is something you can do in the midst of your struggles to fulfill destiny. When trials and pressures come, seeking to destroy your journey, or your adversary seeks to disillusion you with well-thought-out schemes and attacks, you can respond with confidence. Paul's question may be misleading. The actual meaning of the word *if* does not bring into question the possibility that "maybe God is not for us." Rather, it declares the intent that "forasmuch as God is for us!" He is on our side! When we know for certain that He is *for us,* then it matters not the size or strength of our adversaries.

They will all fade in the light of His power and might. Our enemies become His enemies!

There is a cry being heard today across the nations: "We are ready for something more. We are hungry for more!" The status quo will never satisfy the heart of an individual who is passionate about pursuing God and His divine purpose. Desire for your life to count for something. In every human soul there is a desire to be a part of something bigger than earthly achievements or personal goals. Your aspiration becomes *greatness*...not the earthly fame that a championship or promotion can give. This year's champion will soon be forgotten in the wake of this year's heroes! At some point, the nameplate of the one who is your successor will replace the nameplate on your office door. Long for the ability to touch the heart of God and, out of that relationship, count the cost for the price of greatness.

chapter eleven

On Becoming Producers

"What do you want to be when you grow up?" That is the question each of us is asked so often as children. How optimistic we become as we dream about what our lives can be. We answer simply: "A doctor..." "A professional football player..." "A musician..." "A mechanic like my daddy." But as children, we are never really aware that destiny's time clock is ticking away in our hearts.

There are two really awesome moments in everyone's life. The first is when you are born; the second is when you discover why you were born.

How quickly a life can be finished. In Job 14:1, we read, "Man that is born of a woman is of few days" (KJV). Job understood the frailty of human life. Solomon, a man of fame and position, chimed in with his perspective: "Vanity of vanities; all is vanity" (Eccles. 1:2, KJV). He understood that prestige, wealth and recognition were not enough to create a fulfilling life.

Life can be fleeting, its day soon carried away on the wings of time. While passing through the green rolling hills of Fairview, the place where they chose to lay my grandfather to rest, I noticed his headstone. The marker read:

John Lloyd Miller

1899–1976

It was amazing to me that the story of an entire lifetime could be told with a dash. Seventy-seven years of learning to live by faith, of seeing the grace of God enable a man to declare, "When I am weak, then am I strong." A lifetime of trials and victories, tears and celebrations—all marked with an en dash: 1899–1976.

The words over the entrance into the Sunday school wing of the church I attended as a child declared: "Only one life, 'twill soon be past; only what's done for Christ will last." Week after week as I passed through the doorway I would look up and read those words. In order to fulfill the journey to significance, you must walk through the doorway of destiny with a determination to focus on those things that last.

What does it mean to have a sense of destiny? Does everyone have one? How can you tell when God is revealing a part of your destiny to you? When is significance realized?

Destiny awareness can best be described as an inner

conviction that God is at work developing and preparing you to accomplish His specially designed purpose for you during your lifetime. It is the persuasion that your life was meant to produce fruit, not to become famous, for His glory. While others battle over prominence, the person of destiny is aware that significance is of paramount importance in God's kingdom. Our destiny is something we *discover*, not create. You were already a thought in the mind of God long before you were a baby in your mother's womb.

> Declaring the end from the beginning
> And from ancient times things which have not
> been done,
> Saying, "My purpose will be established,
> And I will accomplish all My good pleasure."
> —ISAIAH 46:10, NAS

God knows what He was doing from the beginning. The God of heaven and earth, Jehovah, who manifested Himself through His Son, Christ Jesus, is the only god to make such a declaration. Muhammad can't say the same thing Isaiah said about God. The occultist of our day can't say it. But God declares loudly, "I know the end from the beginning." That means that *God never starts until He is finished!*

OUR DESTINY IS SOMETHING WE DISCOVER, NOT CREATE.

Our lives often take turns that seem out of place or that make no sense. However, if you will acknowledge the Lord in the midst of your struggle to understand, you will find out that it is He who has been directing your steps.

The key to discovering your pathway is to "seek first the kingdom of God..." (Matt. 6:33). The Lord Himself is our pursuit!

David was a pursuer of God, a "God chaser"! It was in his pursuit of God's presence that he became aware of God's plan for his life. Far too often we spend wasted years trying to figure out the plan, while all along the call has been to know the Man, Christ Jesus. If we find Him, we will find His will. David continued pursuing God through his disappointments and failures. He refused to quit in the face of obstacles and opposition. He learned how to encourage himself when everyone around him sought his demise and walked away from him. His sense of destiny kept him full of hope when his boss, tormented by evil spirits, wanted to eliminate him. He learned how to forge relationships, work with difficult people and demonstrate mercy to those who were not as gifted as he in order to accomplish the greater goals. And because of his resiliency, he became the king of all of Israel.

SUCCESS CAN BE MORE DIFFICULT THAN FAILURE IF YOU HAVEN'T BEEN PROCESSED FOR IT.

In the process of becoming king, David defeated all his enemies and brought peace to Israel. The prophetic utterance to him concerning his seed and the "throne of David" become a picture of his significance in God's plan and God's intention. David finally came to Jerusalem and set the ark of God on Zion, a hill overlooking the city of

David. It was not a quick journey, but rather one of determined faith and complete trust. After all the years, David
was now reigning as king, ruler of all of Israel.

It is important to learn how to be *faithful in reigning!*
Success can be more difficult than failure if you haven't
been processed for it. That is why people who have
attained great status due to their *talent*, rather than their
character, are vulnerable to distractions. They are also vulnerable to deceptive people who have the potential of
destroying their futures by abusing those talents. Often
when great status comes as a result of talent, the journey is
so quick that the building blocks of greatness have no time
to be formed. Even David, after killing Goliath, had to
return to the sheepfold and learn continued faithfulness.
Jesus, after confounding the scholars in the temple for three
days, went home with His parents and "was subject to
them," learning obedience (Luke 2:51; Heb. 5:8).

Several key characteristics can be observed in individuals
who desire to make significant contributions in their generation. While we may not include them all here, it is important that we look at a few.

Consumers vs. Producers

Every person on our planet falls into one category or the
other. We are either a consumer or a producer. We live to
get, or we live to give. Those who find a major place of significance choose to give rather than just receive. People are
not remembered in history for what they were given, but
rather for what they gave.

In John 15:8, Jesus said that our heavenly Father is glorified when we bear fruit. God demonstrates who He is by the

fruit we produce in our lives. We are called to be producers!

If your life is going to impact others for God, you must strike a deathblow to the pervasive mentality today that asserts we are just here to hoard up material gain. A man's life is not valued by what he owns. It is more than that! You are not the house you live in or the job you hold. You are a person of great value who has been bought with a great price (1 Cor. 6:20; 7:23). You have eternity beating in your heart (Eccles. 3:11). There is a purpose for your being. No one can take your place or be better at being you than you!

SUCCESS IS NEVER MEANT FOR US ALONE! IT IS A TOOL... A PLATFORM...FROM WHICH WE CAN HELP OTHERS.

God has a bigger plan for your life than just for you to work forty hours a week, going through the mundane routine of merely tolerating your job to get a paycheck and then coming home to spend your evenings watching television. That is not God's glorious plan for your life! There is more! You were born to produce.

The most destitute places in America are the inner cities of our great nation. Yet, the inner cities are not void of talent, abilities, intelligence or creativity. In fact, quite the contrary is true. Many of the gifted artists of our day have come from the neighborhoods that are being ransacked by crime and addiction. Some of the greatest athletes in our history have survived the adolescence of temptation to become successful and prosperous. The cry coming out of the land is, "Give something back!"

While we are all moved with emotion at the stories of young men and women who make something of their lives in spite of difficult circumstances, it is important that we teach them to become more than just consumers. Success is never meant for us alone! It is a tool...a platform... from which we can help others. That is when our success begins to build a bridge into significance.

Rights vs. Responsibility

The battle of the ages has been over rights—the merit of human rights and the dignity of every human life. The rights of the unborn, of women to excel and be promoted to equal status and pay, of the media to express itself—all are all foundational elements to our way of life. However, the journey to significance is not lined with signage that constantly advertises our rights!

Success and accomplishment have privileges and rewards, as well they should. The Bible teaches plainly that rewards are not for everyone—they are for those who overcome. When an individual makes the choice to study, learn and beat the odds against him or her—and win—it is only proper for rewards to be given. However, life at the top also demands a new level of responsibility.

Producers are responsible people. They recognize that they have been blessed to be a blessing. What has come to them has come for the benefit of those around them and not just themselves.

> God has given gifts to each of you from his great variety of spiritual gifts. Manage them well so that God's generosity can flow through you.
>
> —1 PETER 4:10, NLT

In *The Message* translation of this verse in 1 Peter, we read: "Be generous with the different things God gave you, passing them around so all get in on it." To successfully impact your generation, you must be willing to die to yourself and to your craving for position without responsibility. Jesus taught:

> The Spirit of the LORD is upon Me, because He has anointed Me to preach the gospel to the poor; He has sent Me to heal the brokenhearted, to proclaim liberty to the captives and recovery of sight to the blind, to set at liberty those who are oppressed; to proclaim the acceptable year of the LORD.
>
> —LUKE 4:18–19

He was teaching us that the anointing always comes to serve. While you enjoy the effects of the anointing on your life, remember that you have been entrusted with supernatural power to serve your generation effectively and responsibly.

Last year I spoke at a major conference in Nairobi, which was being held for leaders from various African nations. While I was there I had a chance to begin a relationship with one of the other speakers, Ben Wong, a tremendous man of God from Hong Kong. Ben is a director for the cell church network throughout the world. The conference took place only a few months after the September 11 terrorist attack in the United States. It was quite interesting to be challenged by another perspective.

As we talked, Ben would remind me of the mandate and responsibility we have as believers to take what we have been given and use it to serve the Lord and to reach the harvest fields of the world. We in the West have enjoyed an abundance of provisions and resources. We are blessed. The challenge is to become a blessing!

One day at lunch, Ben asked me, "When is enough, enough? I don't have a problem with people prospering," he told me. "However, I believe God is giving them the resources they have for a purpose. My question is, When do you have enough? Is it after two cars...three...a lake house or mountain cabin? Is it when your salary reaches six figures? Whatever you need is fine, but when do you stop consuming it and start using it to be a blessing?" My heart was stirred.

I recognized that as a Christian I have a responsibility to succeed, not for me, but for Him who called me. My purpose in obtaining resources is to bless the kingdom of God and see it expanded to the four corners of the earth. When I reach a point in my life of having what I need, then it becomes important for me to shift into a higher realm of living and become a responsible producer.

Trust vs. Fear

Trust and fear are opposites. Where one exists, the other is either blocked or absent. If you trust, you will not be afraid of giving yourself away. If you are afraid, you will second-guess all your decisions and forfeit any movement toward significance.

Fear creeps in when doubts are allowed to run freely. When you focus on the worst that can happen, or on what someone else will do, your unguarded mind creates an open door for your adversary to taunt and challenge you.

David learned to confront his fears through worship.

From the end of the earth I will cry to You,
When my heart is overwhelmed;
Lead me to the rock that is higher than I.

—PSALM 61:2

David's cry was to be lifted up to a stable position where his intimidation and anxiety could be eliminated. When fear and timidity try to overtake your life, and pressures seek to push you into a corner and keep you from moving forward, you don't need a new hat or another car. What you need the most is a hiding place where you can find strength and solidarity.

It was in Zion that David finally reached a point of ruling and reigning. He learned that it can be more difficult to be faithful while you are on the top! As he soon found out, arriving at a place of success is not the finish line. Rather, it is the ushering in to a whole new level of challenges and life lessons.

Isaac Newton's Third Law of Motion states that for every action there is an equal and opposite reaction. If we follow his logic, it makes sense that any success you achieve will cause ripple effects. George Bernard Shaw once said, "There are two tragedies in life. One is to lose your heart's desire. The other is to gain it."[1]

Let's look at some of the challenges that success will bring, which, if not properly navigated, can destroy your desire for positively impacting a generation.

A Shift in Identity

Identity is affected in two ways—by how you see yourself, and by how others perceive you. Each time you expand to a new level, your identity is slightly altered.

When you record your first music album, you are no longer just a promising musician—you *are now* a musician with a recording contract. When you are promoted to management, you are no longer an *assistant*; you are a *manager*. Begin a business, and you are no longer a hopeful, *aspiring entrepreneur*; you are a *successful businessman*. You have fulfilled a part of your dream. Something has changed in you and in those around you.

David experienced this same thing. Those who at one time had opposed him now embraced him as their king. Those who once stood afar off in criticism now walked beside him in celebration.

YOUR "BECOMING" IS ALL ABOUT TRANSITIONING. IT IS THE EMERGING OF A NEW IDENTITY.

Frequently we hear of those who have reached a plateau of success only to find out that their marriage or key relationships are about to break apart. What happened? There are, of course, many reasons why that can happen, but success, when not handled well, can shake up or even destroy the infrastructure of your life.

That's what your "becoming" is all about—transitioning. It is the emerging of a new identity, coupled with the foundation of previous anchors, with which you must now learn to deal.

There is another shift that takes place in those around us. Your ability to excel and to accomplish goals can bring out the best *and worst* in the people around you. Your ability to discern their hearts and intentions will be critical to your journey.

Maintaining Integrity

Integrity means doing what is right even when no one is watching. David's great challenge with his personal failures did not surface until he was successful and living in a palace. How easy it is for us to act properly when our days are filled with the constant companionship of associates and aides. The challenge comes when we move into the corner office on the top floor, and no one is watching our every move. Or it comes when we can make decisions that no one can question.

The word *integrity* comes from the root *integer*, which means "whole." To live with integrity means that we align ourselves before God with our whole heart and allow Him to bring wholeness to our lives.

For what do you stand? What values do you embrace? What is the moral character of your life? Does it change with each new environment or friend? Are you willing to compromise your values if it means accelerating your promotion or progress?

David's trouble came when he stayed home and did not carry out the duties that were expected of him. In 2 Samuel 11:1, we see the moment his failure in integrity began: "It happened in the spring of the year, at the time when kings go out to battle, that David sent Joab and his servants with him, and all Israel...but David remained at Jerusalem."

When we fail to be where we are supposed to be when we are supposed to be there, we are setting ourselves up for disaster.

The Snare of Pride and Arrogance

Pride becomes a snare that hinders your effectiveness. People will tolerate an arrogant leader for only so long.

You should maintain a healthy respect for yourself, but it is important that you never forget that you have nothing that wasn't given to you by God. Your victories should not create pride; they should create praise. "If it had not been the LORD who was on our side...," who really knows what we would be or where our lives would have gone? (See Psalm 124:1–2.)

We must avoid the trap of thinking, *Now that I am somebody, I can treat people however I want.* If others have belittled you in the past, you may be tempted to belittle those under you once you arrive at a place of success. As a little boy growing up, I remember my father telling me several times, "Son, be sure to treat people kindly on your way up the ladder of success. You may have to pass them on the way down, and you don't want them to bump you off!"

Humility becomes the greatest cure for pride and arrogance. Humbling yourself is never wrong. Power must never corrupt us in our journey to significance.

Seduced by Greed

Success can be intoxicating! It can leave you wanting more and more and more! The desire to accumulate can become an obsession, causing your desire to fulfill the dreams and visions of your life to take a back seat to *stuff*. When that happens, stupidity has begun to control your life.

Much of the greed of our day was born out of a poverty mentality. Poverty has nothing to do with cash flow—it is a spirit. When poverty rules in the heart of an individual, that person believes that he will "never have enough." Therefore he does everything he can to hang on to what he already has. Whether it involves people greedy with their money or pastors greedy with church members, a poverty spirit binds them in fear and competition.

God is bringing a new breed of people forward in this hour. He is raising up people who know how to reign with Christ *with open hands*. These people do not cling to things—they cling to God! The challenge to you is to be faithful in rulership! That is the challenge to us all.

Tom Peters, my spiritual father and counselor, has ministered to my life for many years. He exemplifies reigning with Christ with open hands. Pastor Tom was an alcoholic who found Jesus and was born again when he was in his twenties. After he accepted the Lord as his Savior, he faithfully attended his local church and began to study the Word of God with a passion to learn. His pastor recognized the call of God on Tom's life and helped him to prepare for a lifetime of ministry.

In 1974, Pastor Tom and his wife moved to Lake Worth, Florida, to pastor a church. The denomination that was the covering for the church threatened to close the church down when he began to pastor there, but eventually the denominational leaders decided to let Pastor Tom have a chance at it. Young and unlearned, but eager to work for the Lord, Tom and his wife began to pastor the church. At the first service they conducted, there were eight people in attendance—four women and four children. But Pastor Tom's determined faith and character would not let him give up. He was faithful with what God had given him as an opportunity, and he built trust with the people who began to come to his services. His teaching inspired vision and action. His life became a testimony of character and integrity.

Soon the church began to experience growth. That growth has continued until today. The church has been one of the fastest-growing churches in the nation, with a membership today of over three thousand members.

I use this story about Pastor Tom Peters as an example for you. Pastor Tom is not flashy or well known, and he does not crave the spotlight. He is a great pastor who nurtures the people God has entrusted to him. His twenty-eight years of steady, persistent effort have resulted in a church that ministers in multiplied nations of the world. That church gives more than 25 percent of all of its income for world harvest.

GOD IS RAISING UP PEOPLE WHO KNOW HOW TO REIGN WITH CHRIST WITH OPEN HANDS.

Another person who is especially close to me is a lady who is one of the strongest people I have ever known. She is a giant of faithfulness and integrity in my eyes and to those who know her. She does not come from a famous family and did not attend a higher institute of learning. In spite of the difficulties she faced in her early years, she fought her way through her disappointments and failures to become a champion of encouragement to those who think they can't make it. Her honesty and transparency allow her to show her scars without embarrassment or fear.

Several years ago when I met her, it was obvious to me that she was on a journey. She had a focus in her eyes and a singleness of purpose in her heart that made me know she was destined for greatness. When trials came that attempted to knock her out of her place, she overcame through discipline and prayer. When needs would arise that no one else would respond to, she always put her hand to the plow.

I have watched her as tears became her companions for the night seasons, yet joy would be her song in the mornings. Somehow she kept finding the grace to get up and keep going. She has demonstrated the principle that you can balance your life according to His plan, thus accomplishing more than you would ever imagine.

Whether it was raising her children, maintaining a household, helping to run a ministry office, leading worship, owning her own business or traveling as a national and international speaker, she has done it all with a sense of purpose and dignity. Her creativity and energy are amazing. She has found a way to be faithful when others have fallen by the wayside. In my mind, she embodies everything this book has talked about.

If you wonder how I know her so well, it is because I married her more than twenty-five years ago. This woman of God is my wife, Kathy! What a champion!

These two people are producers par excellence! You can become one, too. You can begin from anywhere, and eventually you can arrive at a place of significance if you are willing to make the journey. Leonardo da Vinci once wrote:

> As a well-spent day brings happy sleep, so a well-
> used life brings happy death.

chapter twelve

It's Your Turn Now

T he greatest need of anyone taking a journey is *direction*. Without it life loses its purpose, and energy is wasted as we walk in circles, having much movement, but little productivity. It is important for every sojourner to recognize that what started as a "small beginning" was the entrance into a greater opportunity. You were born for this day!

While I was praying one day, the Holy Spirit signaled the changing of seasons in my life when He spoke these words: "It's your turn now!" I was aware immediately that it was time for me to accept the Spirit's invitation to a new dimension of ministry and living. The dreams of a previous season were now to become the assignments of this new season. All the preparation and waiting had brought me to a convergence of divine destiny and God's timing.

Everything God begins comes in seed form—small beginnings. Your faithfulness in what has been entrusted to you is the avenue to greater responsibility and opportunity for enlargement. When you understand that, then maturity will take you from *shouting over your potential* to the place of *occupying your destiny*.

One of the intercessors in our ministry brought me a note following one of our midweek services recently. She is a very trusted woman of prayer who happens also to be the mayor of our city. She said, "Pastor, the Lord gave me this word today for you." On a piece of paper she had written the Latin word *ocassio*, which translates *favorable opportunity*! My spirit was stirred as I realized the awesome power that comes from recognizing your moment and responding in obedience. Though it may be overwhelming to our finite humanity with all its limitations, it is God's open door into seasons of significance.

> For if you remain completely silent at this time, relief and deliverance will arise for the Jews from another place, but you and your father's house will perish. Yet who knows whether you have come to the kingdom for such a time as this?
>
> —ESTHER 4:14

Mordecai was holding school that day for Queen Esther. The essential lesson that morning was for her to realize that God had given her an opportunity to move from the position of "being blessed" to "becoming a blessing." Esther had been selected from the crowd to become more than a queen. Her journey involved the saving of a nation.

Granted, the destiny of a nation is a far greater weight than many of us may ever have to carry. However, the destinies of individual lives in our generation are totally dependent on our stepping into our place of purpose. How often have we been placed in circumstances that were uncomfortable because God needed a witness there, someone who could bridge the gap between the realization of divine purpose and missed opportunities?

YOUR FAITHFULNESS IN WHAT HAS BEEN ENTRUSTED TO YOU IS THE AVENUE TO GREATER RESPONSIBILITY AND OPPORTUNITY FOR ENLARGEMENT.

Queen Esther had prepared for this day. She had been through the months of preparation, her selection by the king and the uncovering of her enemies' schemes against her and her people. Now Mordecai was warning her that God had not entrusted all those privileges to her just so she could brag about her status. Privilege and blessing are not just to be displayed and collected like souvenirs. God is not impressed with our human grandeur and positioning. When He allows us to ascend to places of greatness, it is so that we can affect change and usher in kingdom dynamics.

Esther's response was to seize the moment, but not without prayer!

Go, gather all the Jews...and fast for me; neither

eat nor drink for three days, night and day…And
so I will go to the king, which is against the law;
and if I perish, I perish!

—ESTHER 4:16

While men can impart wisdom and counsel, only fervent prayer can prepare your heart for the opportunities that come when it is *your time!* The glowing embers of your spirit are fanned into a blazing flame by your intense pursuit of God in the secret place of prayer. Prayer is what sustains the spirit and keeps us from falling beneath the weight of adversity and opposition. Esther not only prayed personally, but she also taught everyone around her to pray.

WHEN GOD ALLOWS US TO ASCEND TO PLACES OF GREATNESS, IT IS SO THAT WE CAN AFFECT CHANGE AND USHER IN KINGDOM DYNAMICS.

It is difficult to accomplish anything in God's kingdom without prayer. Dreams that are fueled only by talent and personality are hard to bear.

After Esther prayed, she acted! She had prepared herself to be brought into the position of being queen; she had taken the counsel of those who had wisdom concerning her destiny; and she prepared her heart in prayer and the hearts of those who were to assist her. Once the king saw someone who was prepared, he granted an audience and an answer!

Be Prepared to Implement Your Dream

Please hear me, loved ones; most dreams do not die in the visionary stage, but rather in implementation. People are not living mediocre lives because they have not heard anything different or because they have not seen anything different. Most often, it is because they refuse to *do* anything different. There is favor available to those who are willing to prepare and act according to purpose. Yes, there may be difficulties. Yes, it may threaten your existence as you know it. But there is a reward to those who dare to move out.

> Those who sow in tears
> Shall reap in joy.
>
> —PSALM 126:5

Greatness has a remarkable thirst! Just as a man who has been forbidden water will do whatever it takes to satisfy his body's demand for water, so an individual who has endured the long wait for *his time* to come will proclaim, "I have come to the kingdom for such a time as this." He will refuse to be denied or put off. He will not be talked out of his purpose by gainsayers, and he will not be distracted by the voices of those in the crowd who mock his passion and desperation.

You may experience tears that water the dreams of your life. Your tears may last for the night season of your struggle, but joy is the reward of the harvester who endures. Everything has a season and a purpose (Eccles. 3:1). It is your season for impact!

Tony and Rosa Rivera, a very special couple who were a part of our church for many years and are still today a part of our ministerial network, were saved during the Catholic Charismatic Renewal. Being Puerto Rican and raised in the Catholic Church, devotion and commitment were a part of their heritage. Once they were born again, both were soon filled with the Holy Spirit and began to share the Good News of Jesus with everyone they met.

Not long after being filled with the Holy Spirit, they began to attend our church. Because they were very quiet people, many did not know the potential that was within their hearts. Yet, their commitment was remarkable. They were faithful not only to our regular services, but to our intercessory times of prayer as well. It was during this time that each of their seven children had a life-changing encounter with Jesus Christ.

Tony was a businessman who owned his own automobile body repair shop. Rosa stayed at home and raised the children. Tony had been a boxer and baseball player, and he raised his children to be athletes. While they were still small, he would teach each one the fundamentals of baseball. Refusing to let them cry or quit, he developed into each of them his desire to win. His competitive nature eventually became a part of their lives, and one by one each became a standout player for our local high school teams. It was Tony's desire for each of his sons to become professional ballplayers.

One morning while we were at an early-morning prayer session, a prophetic minister who is a dear friend was leading our prayer service. Tony and Rosa were seeking after God. In the middle of prayer, my friend pointed to the center aisle of our auditorium and said, "The man standing there in the middle of the aisle...the Spanish man who is the father of all these boys...I have a word from God for you. God says, 'You will do ministry to the south. God is calling you to do a great work, and it will be to the south of here.'" That was a pretty specific word since we lived in South Florida! There was not much left in our nation to the south.

Tony began to weep, and we prayed over the word. Then he returned to work. During the next several months he continued to pray over that word. One day we talked about God's plans for his life. Tony shared a desire with me to do something for the Lord and to work wherever God wanted him to work.

OFTEN WE FAIL TO RECOGNIZE THAT OUR WAITING TIME IS NOT WASTED TIME; IT IS GOD'S SEASON TO INCUBATE GREATNESS AND TO CLARIFY OUR FOCUS.

Not long after that, Tony and Rosa became the pastors of the Spanish department in our local church. Preaching each week and reaching out to those who were limited due to language barriers in our city, they had tremendous success. Soon the work began to grow. People were being saved and set free. Tony continued to work in his body shop, but God was forming a couple of destiny.

Often we fail to recognize that our waiting time is not wasted time; it is God's season to incubate greatness and to clarify our focus.

Soon it became imperative that we release Tony and

Rosa to raise up the Spanish department into its own church. We released them, and they began to pastor the work. Getting up early, long before daylight, Tony would go into the church to pray and seek God for direction and for a message. Having never been formally trained or educated, he had a great dependence on the Holy Spirit for each step he took. His and Rosa's sensitivity to the Spirit became the key to fulfilling God's purpose in their life. The church continued to grow, but soon they were talking to me about a ministry in the "south."

Tony had been to Venezuela where God had moved on his heart. While he was there, he learned of little children who were living in the city garbage dumps. Family members who no longer cared for these children had left them there. They were discarded because of disease or the family's lack of resources to sustain them. Many were left there to die.

As we talked, tears filled his eyes as he explained the fate of these two- and three-year-old children, scratching through garbage trying to find something to eat, their bodies wasting away with malnutrition while their eight- or nine-year-old siblings tried to "raise them." The burden was more than he could bear. Tony had to do something. All that passion that had pushed him in sports and business was now consuming him for a cause greater than himself.

He arranged for the purchase of land for a children's home. I will never forget the day he took me into the bush to show me the property he wanted to buy to build a place for the discarded, forgotten children of Venezuela. There were no roads, no power lines, no running water—nothing but a dream! The property was literally the side of a mountain, running down to a beautiful lake below.

Once work began, Tony refused to quit. He had to build the roads himself. With a pick and shovel he began to move the side of that mountain. No heavy equipment was available for use, no construction companies to oversee the work—just one man and his wife and a mandate to change someone's life, one wheelbarrow at a time.

ONE OF THE GREATEST DEFINITIONS OF MINISTRY IS THE DESIRE TO IMPROVE SOMEONE'S LIFE.

Tony and Rosa reminded me of the household of Stephanas that Paul wrote about in 1 Corinthians 16. He said, "...they have *addicted themselves* to the ministry" (v. 15, KJV, emphasis added)! They had an *addiction*! An addiction is a strong craving that individuals go to any length to satisfy. Drug addicts or alcoholics spend what they have—even what they don't have—to get what they are craving, never taking into consideration the aftereffects of their actions. Paul said Stephanas and his household had become addicted—not to a controlling substance, but rather to ministry. That became true of Tony and Rosa.

One of the greatest definitions of ministry is *the desire to improve someone's life*. When someone is addicted to ministry, that person has a *strong craving that will spend whatever it has to spend for the opportunity to improve someone else's life!*

After spending many nights sleeping in a small, temporary shack, Tony was able to clear the land for the first children's home to be built. Because of the danger, Rosa stayed at home in Florida praying while Tony broke open the land and obtained the permits from the authorities to build. Nothing kept him from moving forward—not the bandits who sought to steal his few tools, the separation from his wife or the hard work. Making the concrete blocks and constructing the home by himself with only a few volunteers to assist, he was able to build a home for thirty children he would soon rescue from the garbage dump.

I will never forget the first time I visited the home. Our team bought bicycles for the children to ride. When we drove up to the home, smiling, healthy children ran out to meet us as we came through the gate. The joy on their faces brought tears to my eyes as I reflected over the price that had been paid to get them to this place of safety. Had it not been for an automobile body mechanic who refused to live selfishly, many of those little children would have been dead. Instead, today they are being raised in a godly environment, they are given a good education (our ministry helps raise the monies for teachers at the children's home), and they are provided for in every physical way necessary. Who knows, one day the president of that nation may come from that children's home, especially since the children at the home are receiving a consistent education while much of the nation is experiencing violence and inconsistencies.

With one of her sons, Rosa continues to pastor the church in Florida. She travels all over Latin America preaching and praying for miracles in people's lives. Two of their sons are involved in pastoral ministry, and all their children are actively involved in their local churches.

You may never see their names in leading Christian magazines or on television, but then that would not be their focus. When your desire is to do something that will improve someone's life, prominence is not the driving force of your life. This journey is about significance!

YOU NEVER JUST "HAPPEN." YOU ARE NOT A WEED. YOUR LIFE HAS BEEN DIVINELY ARRANGED WITH SPECIFICITY.

Only a small amount of people will ever hear someone say, "You are well known." But multitudes can one day hear the Lord of the Harvest say, "Well done!"

It is your time! It is not enough to know who you are in Christ. You must also know where you are in God's calendar. Be one who is "planted in the house of the Lord." Then you "shall flourish in the courts of our God" (Ps. 92:13). The blessed man of the first chapter of Psalms does not just grow—he is planted. You never just "happen." You are not a weed. Your life has been divinely arranged with such specificity that you must believe you are in the right place at the right time.

The writer of Hebrews awakens us to this realization when he closes the "Faith Chapter" with some very inspiring, yet sobering words. Hebrews 11:40 says, "...they should not be made *perfect* apart from us" (emphasis added). In this incident, the word *perfect* is used to mean "brought to completion." In other words, all the people written about in Hebrews 11 can never complete what they started without us. That is why Hebrews 12 begins with,

"... run with endurance the race that is set before us."

The history of Christianity in the earth is likened to a race in which we all participate. While most believers understand that the Christian race of faith is not a sprint that can be finished in moments, we fail to realize that it is more than a marathon. Marathons can be run alone, without any attachment to others. However, our pathway of purpose is continually tied to others, particularly those who came before us and those who will come after us.

We are running a *relay race*. Every character in Hebrews 11—Abraham, Moses, Joseph, David, the New Testament saints, the apostles, the martyrs—they all ran their "leg" and then passed the baton to someone else. Having completed their turn, they take their places in the grandstands of heaven—"the great cloud of witnesses"—and become cheerleaders for those of us who are still running our leg! They want us to win because, without us, they never get to the finish.

It is mind boggling to realize that no rewards have been passed out as of yet. I know that we hear things said at funerals about the dear departed saint who has "gone on to his reward." While the reward is secure, it is not yet given. No one passes out the awards until the race is over! It would be foolish for us to think that the gold medal would be handed out after the third leg of a four-by-four-hundred relay. Moses needs me! Paul is counting on me to finish my part so that the race is brought to completion! Without us, they cannot be made perfect!

Guidelines for Running the Race

In order to be successful, seize the day and step into your

destiny, you must acknowledge the guidelines for running.

Lay aside the weights.

It is important to put off those things that are going to hinder your ability to perform to the highest of standards. Weights are not necessarily sinful things, but rather those things that drain your energy and slow your performance.

In practice sessions, it is not unusual for athletes to carry weights to build their stamina and build up their muscles. However, when it comes game day, the weights come off so that quickness and response time can be at its optimum level. Far too often our response time to God's invitations is delayed by the "weights" that have our attention, draining us of our productivity.

The challenge is to rid yourself of all the stuff that you have accumulated that is unnecessary to your destiny. We have a tendency to pick up "baggage" as we travel through life, causing us to hesitate at the crossroads of opportunity. Overscheduled lives, divided focus, self-centered indebtedness—all are the result of being caught up in the materialism of your day rather than guarding your ability to respond to destiny's knock at the door. Many people have allowed the "lust of the eyes" to pull them into mortgaging their future for the temporary satisfaction of possessing some status symbol of modern-day success. Possessions are not wrong. But if you have no ability to *delay your gratification,* then you will jeopardize your journey and become weighted down with the "cares of life." Jesus said that those cares would "choke" the life out of your dream seeds.

Michael Jordan is one of the greatest basketball players in history—especially when there are just seconds left in a game. The key to his greatness is not just his ability to make a shot under the pressure of the closing seconds of a game. His greatness rests in his ability to *get open to take the shot!*

Lots of folks can make the shot that wins the game. But so many do not know how to get "open" for the opportunity to take the shot. Learn to put yourself in a position to be used by God. Get open for the shot!

It may be difficult at first to put off some weight. When we try to learn new exercise routines, our natural bodies resist our training efforts when we begin, yet the effort is rewarding. I once heard a military slogan that said, "If you sweat in the peace, you won't bleed in the war!" Get the weight off!

LEARN TO PUT YOURSELF IN A POSITION TO BE USED BY GOD. GET OPEN FOR THE SHOT!

Get rid of begetting sins.

Begetting sins are those things that continue to recur and that steal your confidence and cause you to live in condemnation. For most people, the problem is not some major failure that hinders their journey to significance. Rather, it is the "little foxes" that continue to destroy the vines of our productivity (Song of Sol. 2:15). It is those habits that we cannot seem to overcome and that rise up at just the moment we purpose in our heart to pursue the plans that God has for us, pulling us into ineffectiveness.

Demas forsook Paul and his destiny, having "loved this present world" (2 Tim. 4:10). Something in Demas could never quite let go of the world, and because of it, he lost his direction.

Recognize your propensity for sin. You don't really have to go looking for it; through your natural flesh it comes looking for you. But you have been given the ability through the power of the indwelling Christ to resist every temptation that comes your way and to live free by the blood of Jesus. Don't get arrogant and believe that just because you are now *clean*, you can never get dirty! Walk in humility with a grateful heart for what God has accomplished in your life. It is Christ living in you that enables you to live free from besetting sins (Gal. 2:20).

Run with patience.

Don't get in a hurry. The season of opportunity is moving toward you. There should be celebration in your heart that "faith and patience" are going to allow you to inherit the promise (Heb. 6:12). Don't get sluggish or apathetic in your progress. As you look back over the days of your obscurity to the time when you were plowing and fertilizing your dream, and no one cared, begin to thank God that you are still here. You are a testimony to His sustaining power. Many others have not survived your testimony.

God has begun a good work in you. Don't allow impatience to short-circuit God's plan and drive you ahead of His schedule. Many years ago one of my mentors gave me some very valuable advice when he said, "The Holy Spirit will never give you a spirit of impatience." His words were not what I wanted to hear, but nonetheless true!

Look at Jesus.

We will never complete this journey by looking anywhere or in any direction but directly at Jesus. He is our example, our hope and our strength.

When athletes run a relay race, it is tempting to look

from side to side to see where everyone else is and to judge your own chances of winning. However, every good coach will teach a runner to keep his eyes on the finish line and to not worry about where everyone else is. Every time you turn to see where others are in order to evaluate your own progress, you lose valuable time. Many times it can the difference between winning and losing.

ARE YOU READY? ALL THAT YOU HAVE PRAYED FOR AND BELIEVED FOR IS ABOUT TO EMERGE.

Develop spiritual blinders, the kind that will keep your eyes from wandering off Jesus. The excitement of what is just before you should have your heart pounding with anticipation. You are about to step into the greatest harvest of your life. The enemy knows you are a person of unlimited potential. That is why he has sought to abort your dreams and hinder your journey. He realizes it is your time!

A powerful prophetic moment is about to happen in your life. Are you ready? All that you have prayed for and believed for is about to emerge. Are you ready for the word of the Lord that has been spoken into your life to manifest itself? Get your mind ready. No more "one day" or "some day"—it's *today!*

Purpose in your heart that you are not going to read the stories of others and what they did and wish it were you. Make up your mind that you are going to fulfill your destiny. You were meant to be alive at this particular moment in history!

Just as the voice of the Lord said to Sarah, the Lord is

saying to you, "Don't laugh." He knows that your barrenness has lasted a long time. He knows that you have had
activity, but no *productivity*. Don't laugh! He saw your
schemes to try and force it ahead of time. He watched as
you cried yourself to sleep wondering when the promise
would ever come to pass. The journey through the
mountains and valleys is about to make a new turn. That's
right... *it's your turn—NOW!*

chapter two: "Come Up Here"

1. Source retrieved on the Internet October 30, 2002 from QuoteWorld.org: www.quoteworld.org. Also from Famous Quotes, www.brainyquote.com.

2. Stephen E. Ambrose, *Undaunted Courage* (New York: Simon and Schuster, 1996).

chapter four: Qualified to Be Multiplied

1. T. D. Jakes, *Can You Stand to Be Blessed?* (Shippensburg, PA: Destiny Image, 1995).

chapter six: Becoming a Giant Killer

1. Source retrieved from the Internet November 7, 2002: Franklin D. Roosevelt, First Inaugural Address, Saturday, March 4, 1933: www.bartkebt.cin.124.pres49.html.

chapter seven: Learning to Behave in a Cave

1. Richard D. Phillips, *The Heart of an Executive* (New York: Doubleday, 1999).

chapter eight: Built for Connection

1. For more information about the growth plate, see the following web site: mdchoice.com/PT/consumer/growth.asp#TOP.

chapter nine: The Process of Change

1. Leonard Sweet, *SoulSalsa* (Grand Rapids, MI: Zondervan, 2002), 9.

chapter ten: The Price of Greatness

1. From the speech "The Price of Greatness Is Responsibility" given by Sir Winston Churchill at Harvard on September 6, 1943. Source retrieved from the Internet on

November 11, 2002 at www.winstonchurchill.org/ffh-price.htm.

2. Kevin Simpson, "Victim's diaries prophetic," *Denver Post* (October 20, 1999): source retrieved from the Internet November 11, 2002 at http://uss001.infi.net/denver/post/news/shot1020a.htm.

chapter eleven: On Becoming Producers

1. George Bernard Shaw, "Man and Superman" (1903), act IV. Source retrieved from the Internet November 11, 2002 at www.quotationspage.com/quotes/George_Bernard_Shaw/31.

LET YOUR LOVE GROW!

We pray that God has used Tony Miller to touch your heart and change your life! Here are some additional resources from Charisma House that will also take you deeper into an intimate relationship with God...

KISSING THE FACE OF GOD

by Sam Hinn

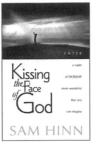

God does not want your worship...He wants YOU!
Let God push you over the edge into that precious zone of familiarity. Discover the kind of love that surrenders you to a lifestyle of intimacy and closeness with the Father.

#536-8   ~~$13.99~~ **NOW $11.19**

EXPERIENCING THE FATHER'S EMBRACE

by Jack Frost

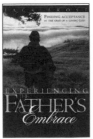

Discover how God's love can ripple through your life!
It's time for the kind of love that changes everything—forever. Forget everything you've ever heard about love, and get ready to experience God's unconditional love.

#845-6   ~~$13.99~~ **NOW $11.19**

Call 1-800-599-5750
AND ORDER THESE LIFE-CHANGING MESSAGES!

Visit our website at WWW.CHARISMAHOUSE.COM and save even more!

Charisma HOUSE

Or visit your local bookstore!

DABP13
2792

Your Walk With God Can Be Even Deeper...

With *Charisma* magazine, you'll be informed and inspired by the features and stories about what the Holy Spirit is doing in the lives of believers today.

Each issue:
- Brings you exclusive world-wide reports to rejoice over.
- Keeps you informed on the latest news from a Christian perspective.
- Includes miracle-filled testimonies to build your faith.
- Gives you access to relevant teaching and exhortation from the most respected Christian leaders of our day.

Call 1-800-829-3346 for 3 FREE trial issues
Offer #A2CCHB

If you like what you see, then pay the invoice of $22.97 (**saving over 51% off the cover price**) and receive 9 more issues (12 in all). Otherwise, write "cancel" on the invoice, return it, and owe nothing.

Experience the Power of Spirit-Led Living

Charisma Offer #A2CCHB
P.O. Box 420234
Palm Coast, Florida 32142-0234
www.charismamag.com

1884A